Nurturing the Spirit

in non-sectarian classrooms

By

Aline D. Wolf

Illustrated by

Joe Servello

Parent Child Press
P.O. Box 675
Hollidaysburg, PA 16648

Dedicated to

four very close friends
with whom I have explored
spiritual questions
for many years

Paula Benjamin, Eadie Kazal, Ruth Robertson
and the late Marilyn Goldberg

Acknowledgements

During the long period of preparing this manuscript some special individuals offered constant encouragement and valuable direction. In particular I want to recognize the work of Joan Gilbert whose year-long project for her C.M.T.E. training course was my original inspiration for this book. I also want to acknowledge the gentle guidance and expert editorial assistance of Paula Benjamin; the many helpful suggestions of Catherine Maresca and Joanne Alex; the enthusiastic interest of Michelle Hartye; the constant understanding and astute assistance of my husband, Jerry, and the versatile support of my associate, Peggy Curran, whose perseverance and expertise made this publication possible.

In addition, I want to thank Dr. Ruth Robertson, Martha Torrence, Marie Riley, Judy Grove, Mary Zajac, Mary Martone, Grace McNally, Ann Marie Swartz, Betsy Coe, Grace O'Connor, Carolyn Patton and Mary Lou Kane who read all or parts of the manuscript and offered helpful comments.

TABLE OF CONTENTS

Preface   i

Part One
The Meaning and Importance of Spirit

Chapter   Page

1   The Spiritual Legacy of Maria Montessori   1
2   What does *Spirituality* Mean?   7
3   The Differences Between *Spirituality* and *Religion*   13
4   Comparing *Spirit* and *Soul*   19
5   The Child — The Essence of Spirituality   27

Part Two
The Spiritually Aware Adult

6   Nourishing the Spirit of the Teacher   33
7   Support For Deepening Spirituality   41
8   Community for Teachers   51

Part Three
Ideas For Children in Non-Sectarian Settings

9   Cultivating Stillness   59
10   Wonder — the Leaven of Spirituality   71
11   Experiencing Wonder in the Classroom   81
12   The Spiritual Meaning of Cosmic Education   89
13   Care of the Earth — A Spiritual Way of Life   99
14   The Spiritual Roots of Peace Education   109
15   Children's Inner Peace and Love   115
16   Peace in the Classroom Community   123
17   The School as a Family / Global Community   133
18   Spirituality and the Arts   143
19   Controlling Advertising in the Environment   151
20   What About God?   157
21   Explaining Spiritual Nurture to Parents   165

Afterword   167

Appendix

A Discussion of Religious Education   173
Catechesis of the Good Shepherd by Catherine Maresca   179

Bibliography and Recommended Resources

PREFACE

The writing of this book over a period of five years has been a personal spiritual journey for me. The more that I delved into what others, wiser and more learned than I, had written about spirituality, the more convinced I became of its ultimate importance in reaching my own full potential as a human being.

Spirituality became not just something to write about or discuss with others; it became something to cultivate more actively in my own life. Meditation, long walks, recollections of my own early childhood experiences, reflections on my strengths and weaknesses as a parent, the sudden death of a very close friend, attending retreats and dwelling on the wonders of nature outside my door brought me to a more intense awareness of this vital part of myself.

For me this re-awakening of my spirit was timely. Now in my sixties, I am experiencing many of the frustrations of growing older. Putting a new emphasis on my spiritual development is helping me to accept more gracefully the discomforts of aging. At this point it seems more important to focus on an actively functioning spirit — a never ceasing sense of wonder, an acceptance of the mistakes I have made and a relinquishing of my obsessive striving for perfection. All this is leading me to a more tranquil acceptance of myself and of others close to me and to an increased sense of oneness with all creation.

I am not implying that I have arrived at the spiritual heights. I am still very much on the journey and might always be, but that journey has a fresh importance in my life. I feel a new excitement about the ultimate questions and the meaning of existence.

Writing this book was a challenge as I did not know if I could do justice to this difficult topic. I knew only that I wanted to reiterate for the followers of Maria Montessori the fundamental purpose of her educational method — to bring about a better world by nurturing the spirit of the child. When writing Parts One and Two of the book, I consulted many published authorities to verify the importance of nurturing the spirit. In Part Three I drew extensively on the experiences of active teachers — Montessorians and others — for everyday examples of nurturing spirituality in their classrooms.

Unlike the teaching of academic subjects, spiritual nurturing cannot be approached with detailed steps that tell the teacher exactly how to present specific concepts with appropriate materials. The effort to nurture the spirit must flow freely from the teacher's own inner essence and from his or her belief that each child is truly a spiritual being. Therefore Part Three is not a typical "how to" manual; particular ages of children are not specified and there are no exact formulas. Rather it describes a variety of spiritually nurturing activities that some particularly aware teachers from various parts of the United States are using in their classrooms. Readers can choose those they feel will work in their own teaching situation and adapt them for the age group in their care.

Because, de facto, most Montessori classrooms are non-sectarian, Part Three, the largest section of this book, includes suggestions that are appropriate for all children in this setting. The ideas, however, are not only for non-sectarian schools; they can also be used as a basic spiritual foundation for children who are in various religiously affiliated programs. A discussion of religious education for children can be found in the Appendix with a detailed example of a Montessori-based Christian religious education program.

I am very grateful to all the teachers who contributed to this book. It is my hope that their work will inspire additional creative ideas for this endeavor and that ultimately all the meaningful activities of spiritually

ii

aware Montessori teachers will be shared in future books, articles, workshops and seminars.

Many of you, my readers, may be devoutly religious, many may have a casual commitment to a particular faith and many others may profess no ties at all to an organized religion. But all of you, I believe, are in one stage or another of making your spiritual journey. My hope is that this book and the spiritual activities that it suggests will bring you further along on your own journey and inspire you to nurture carefully the delicate spirit of each child in your care.

Aline D. Wolf
Hollidaysburg, PA
March, 1996

This book was written mainly for Montessori teachers. However, many readers — both Montessorians and others — who reviewed it in manuscript form believe that it can be useful for any parents or teachers who want to include the spiritual dimension in their care of young children, no matter what methods of education they employ.

Part One

The Meaning
and
Importance of Spirit

Chapter 1

THE SPIRITUAL LEGACY OF MARIA MONTESSORI

Written in Italian on a commemorative tablet at the Montessori family grave in Rome are these words:

Maria Montessori
1870-1952

Famous scientist and pedagogue
who dedicated her entire life to the
spiritual renewal and to the progress
of humanity through the child.
She rests in the Catholic cemetery
Noordwijk (Holland) far away from the
country she had so profoundly loved, far
from her loved ones buried here. This she
decided, to give testimony to the universality of
her work, which made her a citizen of the world.

The phrase, "spiritual renewal and progress of humanity through the child" is indicative, I believe, of what Maria Montessori felt was the essential task of her life.

Universally she is renowned as a physician who became an educational innovator — a woman who removed rigid benches from classrooms and replaced them with small movable tables and chairs. In this comfortable environment, filled with ingenious materials of her own design, she invited children, ages three through six, to select work according to their own interests, thus taking advantage of their individual sensitive periods for learning. The teacher, who had formerly been seen as the source of all knowledge and discipline in the classroom, became a gentle guide who prepared the environment, intensely observed each child, demonstrated the materials that the children had individually chosen and encouraged the children in self-discipline.

This is how the world knows Montessori, but how many know that behind all her educational efforts was her continuous desire to reform humanity — to uncover the true nature of the child — in order, ultimately, to bring peace and harmony to the world? "The child is endowed with an inner power that can guide us to a more luminous future," she wrote. "Education should no longer be mostly imparting of knowledge, but must take a new path, seeking the release of human potentialities."[1]

It is not surprising that many parents and educators know Montessori primarily through her academic materials. This equipment can be examined, explained and, above all, manipulated. Beautiful wooden replicas of Montessori's tower of cubes, sound boxes, sandpaper letters, counting rods, puzzle maps and many other materials are still used daily in thousands of Montessori schools almost a century after she first crafted them.

Far less known are her theories about cultivating the spiritual nature of the child. These theories have no concrete form; they cannot be handled. Yet her writings about the spiritual nature of the child are fundamental to all of Montessori's educational work.

In an article entitled "The Spiritual Development of the Child", Sofia Cavalletti, a religious educator of young children in Rome, wrote, "As Montessorians, I think, we contradict ourselves if we do not satisfy the child's thirst for the transcendent, his most basic need. We prevent the method from fully attaining its aim: the harmonious living of people. The Montessori Method...[by] its very nature is spiritual and we violate its nature if we deprive it of its full spiritual blossoming."[2]

---

[1] Maria Montessori, *Education For a New World*, p. 2.

[2] Sofia Cavalletti, "The Spiritual Development of the Child," *Montessori Talks to Parents*, Series One, Number Three, p. 14.

Why then is the nurturing of the child's spirit such an elusive element in so many Montessori schools? Spiritual development is rarely mentioned in school brochures or in assessments of a child's work. At conferences parents will ask, "Is she learning her sounds?" or "What materials is he using to learn math?" Only rarely will a parent ask a question touching on the child's spiritual growth.

To say that spirituality is generally elusive in Montessori circles does not say that it is not present in many Montessori classrooms. It is present in widely varying degrees of intensity but it is not usually obvious to the casual observer. Administrators often find difficulty in writing about the spiritual aspect of their work in a mission statement or in school publicity. Nurturing the child's spirit cannot be demonstrated to parents in the same way that the moveable alphabet or golden beads can be used as illustrations of hands-on academic activities.

Specific means of nurturing the child's spirit are elusive even in Montessori's own writings. There is no doubt that the word *spirit* is everywhere in her writings. Typical of many such passages without specific details are these words — "We must help the child to act for himself, will for himself, think for himself; this is the art of those who aspire to serve the spirit. It is the teacher's joy to welcome the manifestations of the spirit."[3]

In optimum situations such passages translate into the special attitudes of spiritually-aware Montessori teachers. Other Montessori teachers find it difficult to reach this spiritual level. Perhaps it is not emphasized enough in some Montessori training courses; also Montessori's own writings on nurturing the spirit are non-specific in contrast to her detailed descriptions of academic exercises.

Another reason that the spiritual dimension of Montessori's work has been downplayed in the United States is that the majority of the Montessori schools are non-sectarian. As such, their student bodies reflect the religious diversity of this country. Even in small cities the enrollment in a Montessori class can include a wide variety of persuasions — Protestants, Jews, Catholics, Unitarians, atheists, Buddhists,

---

[3] Maria Montessori, *Education For a New World*, p. 89.

Muslims, Hindus and others. Because of the sensitivity of many parents to any kind of sectarian influence, most teachers go out of their way to refrain from activities that might be interpreted as religious.

Although nurturing the child's spirit is very different from teaching a specific religion, the distinction, which will be discussed in Chapter 3, is not always clear. Therefore some Montessori teachers, rightly convinced that religious training is the prerogative of each individual family, have backed off and left unexplored many avenues of nurturing the child's spirit. Sadly this misunderstanding of terms may have weakened and sometimes eliminated the spiritual element that Montessori felt was basic to her educational philosophy.

In *Peace and Education* Montessori wrote, "If education recognizes the intrinsic value of the child's personality and provides an environment suited to spiritual growth, we have the revelation of an entirely new child, whose astonishing characteristics can eventually contribute to the betterment of the world."[4] Now that thousands of children who attended Montessori schools have become adults in the very active years of their lives, we have to ask ourselves the tough questions about what they are doing to carry out her objective. Can they be distinguished from those adults who are interested only in personal satisfaction or materialistic gain? Are they working actively for care of the earth, peace, justice for minority groups, help for third world countries or educational reform? How are they nurturing their own children? Ultimately we can measure the success of Montessori's approach only by observing our graduates.

In 1948 Montessori wrote, "If education is always to be conceived [as] a mere transmission of knowledge, there is little to be hoped from it in the bettering of man's future. For what is the use of transmitting knowledge if the individual's total development lags behind?...

"The child is endowed with unknown powers, which can guide us to a radiant future. If what we really want is a new world, then education must take as its aim the development of these hidden possibilities."[5]

When we read these words of Montessori today, do we skip over them lightly as if they were an impractical fantasy that is no longer

[4] Maria Montessori, *Peace and Education*, pp. 20-21.

[5] Maria Montessori, *The Absorbent Mind*, pp. 3-4.

viable? Or do we read them as the most important thrust of her life's work that is yet to be realized? There is no doubt in my mind that the "psychic entity," "unknown powers" and "hidden possibilities" of which she speaks are deeply rooted in each child's spirit. I feel it is time to give renewed attention to this spiritual legacy that may reveal the most important and far-reaching implication of Montessori education.

Chapter 2

WHAT DOES *SPIRITUALITY* MEAN?

In light of the original basic importance of nurturing the spirit in Montessori education, I believe that present Montessorians of all ages and from all cultures must take time for serious reflection on the meaning of the word *spirit* and its derivatives, *spiritual* and *spirituality*. We must take these words and wrestle with them, examine their nuances and determine their many meanings.

Spirituality is rooted in the most profound depths of each human being, in all nature and in the universe that surrounds us. Even though it animates all of life, the essence of spirituality is difficult to comprehend because it cannot be perceived by our physical senses or proven by our intellectual powers. We use our physical senses to experience the physical world and our mental powers to access ideas, but spirituality eludes these faculties. While it manifests itself in a person's mental and physical activities, the spirit itself cannot be seen, heard, touched, analyzed or proven. Yet from the dawn of civilization, some form of spirituality has been inherent in every culture that is known.

Spirituality does not even lend itself readily to a dictionary definition. In Webster's Unabridged Dictionary (Third New International) the first of many definitions of *spirit* is "the breath of life: the animating or vital principle giving life to physical organisms." It is derived from the Latin word *spirare* that means *to breathe*. While this definition highlights the supreme importance of spirit as the life-giving principle of our world, it does not enable us to fathom its essence in relation to our everyday experiences.

It is interesting and useful, I believe, to read and compare the interpretations of other thinkers who have pondered this enigmatic term:

Jean Grasso Fitzpatrick, whose books are addressed to parents, writes, "The word *spiritual* refers to an awareness of our sacred connection with all of life. Our spirituality is our opening to one another as whole human beings, each different and precious, and our exploring how we can truly learn to love. Day by day it is our learning reverence for our earth and its creatures."[1]

The late Dr. Beverly-Colleene Galyean gave more concrete examples of spirituality, "We all have spiritual experiences such as the feeling of being uplifted, transported beyond ordinary sensory experiences...the awesome sense of oneness with the universe that comes from contemplating the stars or from climbing a high mountain and surveying the vast panorama beneath us, or the ecstatic sense of wonder at the birth of a child...The tendency to make peace rather than war, emphasis on collaborative rather than competitive efforts, and the recognition of common needs experienced by people of every culture and creed...These are all aspects of spirituality."[2]

Also in many areas that were not influenced by European culture, spirituality has a singular importance in relation to nature. The Faithkeeper of the Onondaga Nation of Native Americans, states, "Spirituality is the essence of our lives. It's what makes a tree grow and what makes a bird sing. What makes a human smile. Spirituality has its own force and has its own being, something you can't see. It's the power of the universe."[3]

Expressing similar sentiments, an Aboriginal woman writes, "To understand us you have to understand our spirituality. It makes us unique.

---

[1] Jean Grasso Fitzpatrick, *Something More*, p. 7.

[2] Beverly-Collene Galyean, "Honoring the Spirituality of Our Children Without Teaching Religion in the Schools', *Holistic Education Review*, Summer, 1989, p. 24.

[3] M.C. Burns, "Interview with Oren Lyons," *Syracuse Herald Journal*, July 9, 1991.

It shows respect to Mother Earth in thankfulness to God...Our spirituality begins from the day we are born, and continues in how we live, how we care for our brothers and sisters, how we deal with our extended family, and how we care for God's creation. It is all balanced and cannot be divided."[4]

Gang, Lynn and Maver in their writings also maintain that spirituality manifests itself as we experience our relatedness. "This deep connection to creation evolves over our entire life. It may be experienced as special moments when one is alone in the forest, or when one stares into the heavens on a star-filled night, or observes cloud formations. It is an experience of awe and wonder and an awareness of the oneness of all. Spirituality is the recognition of the inherent beauty, truth and goodness in life. It calls forth such traits as compassion, joy and humility."[5]

Recognizing that spirituality provides meaning for life, Mary Fisher in her book, *Sleep With The Angels: A Mother Challenges AIDS*, writes, "Spirituality gives us depth. It's where we sink our roots so we can grow. It's what enables us to capture and hold a broad, clear picture of reality — where we can see that we are called to a higher purpose than self-service and self-satisfaction."[6]

Viewing spirituality as an awareness of all that is and an openness to what is not, Leo Buscaglia writes, "Fully functioning persons have a deep sense of spirituality. They know that their personhood and the world in which they live cannot be explained or understood through human experience alone. They know that they must make the 'mystical leap.' They must go beyond themselves, beyond their limited reality. They have an inexplicable sense of something more. They feel a greater operative intellect than their own, even if they are at a loss to give it a name. They are aware of a great design, incessantly operative, in which all is compatible and in which there are no contradictions."[7]

---

[4] Anne Pattell-Gray, *Through Aboriginal Eyes*, pp. 5-6.

[5] Philip S. Gang, Nina Myerhof Lynn, and Dorothy J. Maver, *Conscious Education*, p. 6.

[6] Mary Fisher, *Sleep With The Angels: A Mother Challenges AIDS*, p. 89.

[7] Leo Buscaglia, *Personhood*, p. 118.

Albert Schweitzer, the physician who devoted many years to the care of the poor in Africa, wrote, "Life affirmation is the spiritual act in which man ceases to live unreflectively and begins to devote himself to his life with reverence, in order to raise it to its true value."[8]

Bridging the traditional gap between spirituality and science, Albert Einstein, as quoted by Beverly-Colleene Galyean, wrote, "A spirit is involved in the Laws of the universe — a spirit vastly superior to that of man, and one in the face of which we, with our modest powers, must feel humble."[9]

After reflecting on these quotations, I should like to highlight four aspects of spirituality that emerge from these particular descriptions:

> Spirituality calls us to a sense of awe and
> wonder characterized by a reverence for the
> earth and all its creatures and a desire to
> live in harmony with all of nature.

*   *   *

> In a certain sense, spirituality involves openness
> to an existence that is beyond our sensory and
> intellectual experience. It asks us to take a "mystical
> leap," to transcend our human limitations and to be
> open to the possibility of a vastly superior
> creative spirit in the universe.

*   *   *

> Spirituality fosters a profound humility in human
> beings. It invites us to lead a more reflective exist-
> ence and to contemplate the unfathomable questions.

*   *   *

> Spirituality implies a sacred connection with all of
> life and a oneness with the universe. This means

---

[8] Walt Burnett, Editor, The Human Spirit, pp. 308-309.

[9] *Holistic Education Review*, Summer, 1989, p. 28.

that every act of carelessness, selfishness, indiff-
erence, hatred and violence toward nature or toward
other human beings is actually an act against
ourselves, our families and our culture. Therefore,
spirituality summons us to the highest of human
virtues, such as love, caring, generosity, responsibility
for our actions, forgiveness, compassion and openness
to one another. It leads us to sharing rather than
accumulating, to cooperation rather than competition
and to peace rather than violence.

There are other aspects of spirituality, I am sure. Those listed above
are simply a starting point for further exploration related to non-sectarian education.

Chapter 3

THE DIFFERENCES BETWEEN
SPIRITUALITY AND *RELIGION*

In an article entitled "The Spiritual in the Classroom," Paul Byers, an anthropologist and associate professor of education at Teachers College, Columbia University, laments the confusion that stems from implying that the word *spiritual* means *religious*.

"Religions are particular *answers*," he writes, "to the universal human questions about the creation and meaning of life. Spiritual refers to the universal personal concern for the *questions*. When we removed religion from public education to avoid conflict and allow freedom of religion, we removed the *answers* religions offered. But unfortunately, we also threw out, ignored or denied the perennial *questions*, and education nourished mainly the material aspects of life."[1]

In order for teachers to nourish spirituality in a non-sectarian class-room it is important for them to understand the essential difference between spirituality and religion. Spirituality is a basic quality of human nature; the practice of a particular religion is the way that many people choose to give voice to their spirituality.

The word *religion* refers to a set of beliefs and code of behavior that are accepted by a large group of people and expressed in their traditional prayers, dogmas and rituals. Most religions trace their origin to a particular founder, usually esteemed as a prophet, mystic or divine individual.

---

[1] Paul Byers, "The Spiritual in the Classroom," *Holistic Education Review,* Spring, 1992, p.6.

Belief in "the truth" of the founder's revelations gives rise to various claims of one religion being superior to all others. Those who assume they have "the truth" often feel compelled to convert others to their beliefs. Consequently in the history of the world, most of the wars have been fought, not because of differences in spirituality, but because of differences in religion.

The practice of religion usually fosters devotion to God —or a deity by some other name — and this devotion gives meaning to life. It encourages the practice of virtue and gives comfort in times of sorrow and affliction. Nearly all religions provide their followers with symbols, liturgies, scriptures and/or other sacred writings. Nevertheless spirituality can animate a person's life without these formalized expressions. Often a deeply spiritual person does not belong to a particular organized religion.

Equally true, however, is the fact that this same profound sense of spirituality can be a very strong basis for religious faith — in fact, a basis for any one of the many diverse religions of the world. Authentic spirituality can even cross the boundaries of different faiths. For example, a Christian who finds meaning in his life through a sense of unity with the universe may have more in common with a Buddhist who shares these sentiments than he has with certain fellow Christians for whom religion is only a habit or social obligation.

The authors of *Conscious Education* use the metaphor of the wheel with many spokes to illustrate similarities among various faiths. "In this wheel each spoke represents a different religion. The center of the wheel can be thought of as the Truth (or authentic spirituality). As one proceeds along the path of any spoke towards the center, one gets closer to the ultimate Truth, yet at the same time, one gets closer to every other spoke (religion) as well."[2]

To highlight the virtues that are common to six of the major world religions, the following teachings are often cited for their similarity:

From Buddhism — "Hurt not others in ways that you yourself would find hurtful." (Udana-Varga 5,18).

---

[2] Philip S. Gang, Nina Myerhof Lynn, and Dorothy J. Maver, p. 44.

From Hinduism — "Do not unto others what would cause you pain if done to you." (Mahaoharata 5, 1517).

From Judaism — "What is hateful to you, do not do to others." (Talmud, Shabbat 3 id).

From Taoism — "Regard your neighbor's gain as your own gain and your neighbor's loss as your own loss." (Tai Shang Kan Ying p'ien).

From Christianity — "Do unto others as you would have them do unto you." (Matthew 7:12).

From Islam — "No one of you is a believer until he desires for his brother that which he desires for himself." (Sunnah).[3]

I believe that the essence of this maxim, in any of the above wordings, can serve as the primary base for acquiring all the common virtues: love, compassion, forgiveness, honesty, truthfulness, kindness etc.

Abraham Maslow, the renowned psychologist, urges the teaching of such common core values in non-sectarian classrooms. He writes, "This in no way controverts the American separation of church and state for the simple reason that spiritual, moral and ethical values have nothing to do with any church. Or perhaps, better said, they are the common core of all religions, including the non-theistic ones. It is possible that these ultimate values should be the far goals of all education...An education that leaves untouched the entire region of transcendental thought is an education that has nothing important to say about the meaning of human life."[4]

Montessori herself felt that her Children's House provided a spiritual base for almost any religion. Speaking of the phenomenal success of her early experiments in Rome she described the equally positive reactions of diverse observers — Catholics, Jews and Buddhists. Each saw in the actions of the children the necessary groundwork for the triumph of his own principles.[5]

This was not wishful thinking on the part of Montessori. Her educational method has proven compatible with many religions and cultures.

---

[3] *Christopher News Notes*, #339, November, 1991.

[4] Abraham Maslow, *Religious Values and Peak Experiences*, pp. 57-58.

[5] E. M. Standing, Editor, *The Child in the Church*, p. 4.

While she was confined to India during World War II, Montessori trained many natives of both India and Ceylon (now called Sri Lanka) in her method. The movement took root and teacher training continued even after Montessori returned to Europe in 1946. Beginning in the 1960's, many of these Indian and Ceylonese women immigrated to the United States to fill the need for trained teachers in the resurgence of Montessori education at that time. These Hindu and Buddhist teachers worked amicably with the American leaders of the new Montessori movement, most of whom were Jewish or Christian.

The universality of Montessori is widely recognized. In an article entitled, "Montessori and the Baha'i Faith," Barbara Hacker wrote in 1991, "Like the vast majority of Italians, Montessori was a Catholic. What pervades her writing, however, is not her Catholicism (although she sometimes draws on the lives of the saints or quotes scripture to illustrate a point) but her deep sense of spirituality and her ability to transcend a particular religion for the deeper truth. It was this quality that made her work attractive to people of so many religious backgrounds. Spirituality was at the very heart of her work with children... She spoke with certitude on this subject when it was not fashionable to do so."[6]

In order to encourage teachers to foster spiritual development in today's classroom, several modern educational leaders have clarified its distinction from teaching religion. David Elkind, a professor of child study at Tufts University, writes, "Spirituality can be used in either a narrow sense or a broad one. In the narrow sense spirituality is often used to indicate a particular set of religious beliefs. A person who is devout in these beliefs might be said to be a spiritual person. Spirituality, however, can also be used in a much broader sense. Individuals who, in their everyday lives, exemplify the highest of human qualities such as love, forgiveness, and generosity might also be said to be spiritual. It is spirituality in the broad, non-denominational sense that I believe can be fostered by educational practice."[7]

This distinction is carried further by Beverly-Colleene Galyean. "People who oppose teaching religion in the schools do so because they

---

[6] Barbara Hacker, *NAMTA Journal*, Summer, 1991, p.43

[7] David Elkind, "Spirituality in Education", *Holistic Education Review*, Spring, 1992, p.12.

fear that children will be taught dogma contrary to that lived in the home... The honoring of spirituality, however, is not a debatable issue. Spirituality is not doctrine that is taught. Rather it is a vital energy... that determines how we create meaning in our lives.[8]

In order to fulfill our mission as true Montessorians, we can no longer avoid contending with the distinction between spirituality and religion. It must be the subject of training sessions, staff meetings, workshops, articles, lectures and debates. It is time to tackle the tough questions, such as, "Can we mention God in our classrooms?" It is time to think about how we can reply when a child asks, "Who made the world?" or "Where did my grandmother go when she died?"

As Montessori teachers, we do not have to come into the classroom with answers to the mysteries of life. We, ourselves, do not have to be involved in a particular religion. It is time, however, to be serious about our own spiritual journeys and more aware of their fundamental role in nurturing the delicate spirit of each of the children in our care.

---

[8] *Holistic Education Review,* Summer, 1989, p. 25.

Chapter 4

COMPARING *SPIRIT* AND *SOUL*

While doing research for the preparation of this book, I became aware of a great deal of confusion between the words *soul* and *spirit*. Historically and semantically these terms have been used interchangeably in religious teachings and in literature as well as in Montessori's work. Although some scholars have tried to differentiate between the two words, their meanings continue to overlap in many everyday situations.

Because both of these words refer to immaterial entities, it seems that an absolutely clear distinction cannot be made. Nevertheless, for the purpose of this book, I want to give my own interpretation of their differences in order to make sure that what I consider the spiritual needs of the child are recognized as equally important as those usually referred to as needs of the child's soul or psyche.

This basic confusion between *soul* and *spirit* is complicated by the fact that the word *soul* usually has two different meanings. One is a religious meaning — an animating principle of human beings that has the possibility of living on after death. The other meaning of *soul* — psyche — is a psychological one. As the invisible essence of a human being, the psyche is thought to animate the human body during life and, among other powers, includes intelligence, imagination, emotions, desires and will.

In referring to the immaterial essence of a human being that is believed to live on after death, some religions use *soul* and others use *spirit* to refer to the same entity. For example, many Christians believe that the soul can be defiled by sin and destined for eternal punishment in hell or else made radiant by good deeds and destined for eternal happiness in heaven.

Hindus call this same part of a human being *spirit* or *atman*. Its future, too, in reincarnation is determined by the quality of one's deeds. After a life of sin, the spirit is reborn in a lower caste or lower form of life. Conversely after a life of good deeds the spirit is reborn into a higher level of life.

Webster's Unabridged Dictionary also clearly points out the interchangeable use of these two terms — "Soul and spirit are often convertible terms, especially in their denotation." As an example in literature, the dictionary cites lines from two well known poets. Robert Browning writes, "When my lips just touched your cheek — touch which let my *soul* come through." Alfred Lord Tennyson expresses the same idea with, "And our *spirits* rushed together at the touching of the lips."[1]

In the English translations of Maria Montessori's works it appears that she, too, does not make a clear distinction between *soul* and *spirit*. For example, read the first chapter of *The Absorbent Mind* where the terms seem to be used interchangeably with each other and also with references to *inner powers, hidden possibilities, psychic nature, psychic powers* and *psychic force*. Thus, "Today we are beginning to see the value of these ungathered fruits, more precious than gold, for they are man's own *spirit*." "...they [the children] offered us amazing revelations of the greatness of the human *soul*." "He [the child] has the chance to build up a complete *psychic structure*, before the intelligence of grown-ups can reach his *spirit* and produce changes in it." "We then become witnesses to the development of the human *soul*."[2]

To help clarify this confusion of terms, I wrote to Sofia Cavalletti, a Montessori religious scholar in Rome, asking her if *soul* and *spirit* were used interchangeably in Montessori's original work in Italian.

In her reply Dr. Cavalletti stated, "In the Italian editions the word *soul* (anima) does not seem to appear; anyway it is not characteristic of

---

[1] Webster's New International Dictionary, Second Edition, Unabridged.

[2] Maria Montessori, *The Absorbent Mind*, pp. 3, 4, 7 & 9.

Maria Montessori's writings. The terms she uses are *psiche* (psyche) and *spirito* (spirit). With this last word she means the highest faculties characteristic of the human being, which are not found in other creatures."[3]

In his best selling book, *Care of the Soul*, the psychiatrist, Thomas Moore, never actually gives the reader a definition of soul, although he makes it clear that he is talking about the psyche rather than the infinite soul of organized religions. He writes, "It is impossible to define precisely what the soul is. Definition is an intellectual enterprise anyway; the soul prefers to imagine. We know intuitively that soul has to do with genuineness and depth...soul is not a thing but a quality or dimension of experiencing life and ourselves. It has to do with depth, value, relatedness, heart and personal substance."

Much later in his book, Dr. Moore writes about *spirit*. "In the broadest sense, spirituality is an aspect of any attempt to approach or attend to the invisible factors in life and to transcend the personal, concrete, finite particulars of this world."[4]

In exploring the difference between *soul* and *spirit* two other contemporary writers have been helpful to me. Both use the psychical rather than the religious meaning of soul.

The late Bede Griffiths, an English monk, who spent many years living in an ashram in India writes, "Soul is a psychological organism set between the world of the senses and the world of the spirit...Spirit in man," he continues, "is the point of his communion with the universal spirit which rules and penetrates the whole universe. This is the point of human transcendence, the point at which the finite and the infinite, the temporal and the eternal, the many and the One meet and touch."[5]

The late J.G. Bennett, a former director of research at the Institute for the Comparative Study of History, Philosophy and the Sciences, makes a somewhat similar distinction between *spirit* and *soul* by using the word *psyche*. He writes, "By psyche I mean all that concerns our subjective life, our consciousness of what is happening to us and of what we are

---

[3] Letter to Aline D. Wolf, May 24, 1995.

[4] Thomas Moore, *Care of the Soul*, pp. xi, 5 and 232.

[5] Bede Griffiths, *The Marriage of East and West*, pp. 58 and 76.

doing...Psyche includes sensations, emotions, imagination and thoughts — both conscious and unconscious." The word *spiritual*, on the other hand, "implies that there is a reality that cannot be reached through our senses and which we cannot grasp with our minds."[6]

I feel that *soul* and *spirit* are both intangible and invisible aspects of human nature. The *soul*, however, as a psychological entity, is the more familiar and personal of the two. It is, indeed, the essence of our humanity, expressed in our actions, our relationships, our thinking, feelings, imagination, insights and other psychological powers that are seated in particular areas of the brain. It is also the part of a human being that some believe has the possibility of living on after death.

Spirit by its very nature is much more elusive. No biological or medical researcher has ever found a tangible trace of spirit in a human body. No physical point has been discovered that is in touch with the universe. Even the latest scanning machines, subtle enough to detect by region the activities of the thinking brain, see no sign of even a neuron that could be termed *spirit*. And yet, as J.G. Bennett writes, "Spirit is "the 'I' that is more truly ourselves than the psychic apparatus of thought, feeling and sensation."

I am attempting to make a distinction between *soul* and *spirit* because Montessori teachers must deal with the basic needs of the whole child — body, soul and spirit. I do not mean that we have three separate avenues of approach. Educating the whole child implies a unified holistic approach. But without attempting some distinction there is a danger that the spiritual needs may be neglected. Teachers and/or parents may feel when they have fully addressed the psychological needs that they have adequately taken care of the spiritual needs. This may be one of the reasons why the spiritual needs of children are not always sufficiently met in our classrooms.

The physical needs of children are well known. Air, water, food, shelter, sleep and human contact form the base of Abraham Maslow's famous chart of the Hierarchy of Needs. I like to reword these as unpolluted air, pure water, healthful food, comfortable shelter, undisturbed sleep

---

[6] J. G. Bennett, et. al., *The Spiritual Hunger of the Modern Child*, pp. 2-3.

and loving human contact. Others could be added, such as competent medical care and frequent opportunities for movement.

In recent years, increasing attention is being given to the care and stimulation of the child's psyche. Maslow mentions the need to feel secure, to be loved, to belong and to feel esteemed. We can easily add the need for intellectual stimulation, emotional balance, stimuli for imagination and curiosity, the need to express or assert one's self, to trust, to succeed, the need for socialization and for friendship. There are many others, of course, but this list gives a basic idea of the kinds of needs that are those of the soul when it is defined as *psyche*.

What then are the spiritual needs of children? Immediately I think of the need for some periods of quiet and solitude when they can escape the constant noise of chatter, radio, TV, and listen to the still small voice within. Because the spirits of children are not truly nourished by pre-packaged answers, cold facts or even routine presentations of materials, they need opportunities to ponder some of the mysteries. Children have a right to be nourished spiritually in ways that leave the door open for deeply appropriate responses such as wonder, respect and gratitude. There is the need to find meaning in their lives, the need to question why they are here and why the world exists as it does. Their spirits need reassurance that what they do matters. Their spirits need to know why it is better to act in one way and not in another. In addition there is the need for something beyond themselves and the physical world, the need to connect to the universe, a need that cannot be satisfied except in relation to a Whole, a reality that is more than what they see in their everyday experience.

And so we must constantly address the needs of the whole child. If some of the physical needs are neglected, the child's body may become debilitated and functioning may be hampered in one way or another. If the needs of the soul or psyche are grossly neglected, the child could become an insecure or emotionally immature adult. If spiritual nurturing is neglected the child may become an adult who sees no meaning in life, is bored with life, careless with life, or an adult who is determined to have power, prestige and possessions, without regard for care of the earth, the animal kingdom and/or the welfare of other human beings.

The serious consequences of ignoring the spirit were pointed out by the famous psychoanalyst, Carl Jung, when he revealed that among all his patients over the age of thirty-five, there was not a single one whose problem in its deepest roots was not a spiritual one.[7]

Because so many other books have been devoted to the physical and psychical development of children, the primary focus of this book will be on spiritual nurturing. But it is inevitable that care of the soul and care of the spirit will sometimes overlap. Activities in the classroom may relate to both of these aspects of the whole child as we strive to nurture a fully functioning human being.

---

[7]Carl G. Jung, *Modern Man in Search of a Soul*, p.229.

Chapter 5

THE CHILD — THE ESSENCE OF SPIRITUALITY

In a lecture given in London in 1961, as part of a series entitled *The Spiritual Hunger of the Modern Child*, Mario Montessori, the son of Dr. Maria Montessori, opened his talk by declaring that "I don't believe that the child has a spiritual hunger ... because the child is already the essence of spirituality." He went on to explain that it was the realization of this spirituality which so overwhelmed his mother that she left everything else she had done previously in order to follow the child.

"She had a brilliant career in front of her. She was a young woman doctor in Italy, she was a lecturer at the University of Rome...everyone expected her to have a very successful future in her field."

What was even more remarkable, he continued, was that "Dr. Montessori herself was not particularly religious. On the contrary, at that time science was against religion on the grounds that you cannot prove God's existence, so it must be all nonsense. Dr. Montessori was then a positivist...

"[But] the children...made a great convert: Dr. Montessori, a scientist and a disbeliever...left her career, she left her brilliant position among the socialists and among the feminists, she left the university, she even left the family..." to give her life to nourishing the inner spirit of the child.[1]

Maria Montessori herself describes this conversion experience, "It was January 6, 1906, when the first school [Casa dei Bambini] was opened

---

[1] J. G. Bennett et al., pp. 41-51.

for normal children between three and six years of age...On that day there was nothing to be seen but about fifty wretchedly poor children, rough and shy in manner, many of them crying...entrusted to my care...

"I set to work feeling like a peasant woman who, having set aside a good store of seed-corn, has found a fertile field in which she may freely sow it. But I was wrong. I had hardly turned over the clods of my field when I found gold...the clods concealed a precious treasure. I was not the peasant I had thought myself. Rather I was like foolish Aladdin, who, without knowing it, had in his hand a key that would open hidden treasures."[2]

Montessori had ingeniously provided an environment that, instead of adding spiritual essence to the child's nature, had revealed what was already there. Somehow this spirit had been blocked in other educational situations. Children behaved badly because they lived in conditions in which their spirituality could not express itself. Their spirits rebelled in violence, withdrawal, selfishness and disregard for others. After several months Montessori was truly astonished as she saw these negative characteristics gradually recede in the children in her Casa dei Bambini. At that point she recognized for the first time the true spirit within the child. What was even more remarkable was that the children themselves had helped her to see this. "Not everyone realizes," she wrote, "that the child is a wonderfully precious aid to the adult and that he can...exercise a formative influence on the adult world."[3]

In a beautiful book, *Whole Child/Whole Parent*, Polly Berrien Berends echoes Montessori, "We can see that the baby is as much an instrument of nourishment for us as we are for him. We can foster his growth as a peaceful and loving individual only if we nourish him with love and peace. And we can know love and peace only if this is what we hunger for and feed upon in consciousness. Most of us would do more for our babies than we have ever been willing to do for anyone, even ourselves. In this way the child, seemingly so helpless, performs the mighty work of awakening in us a tremendous appetite for understanding and so brings us to the table of love."[4]

---

[2] Maria Montessori, *The Secret of Childhood*, Orient Longmans, pp. 128-129.

[3] E. M. Standing, Editor, *The Child in the Church*, p. 7.

[4] Polly Berrien Berends, *Whole Child, Whole Parent*, p. 35.

Why is the spirit of the infant so powerful? Is it because it is new, and still close to the universal spirit of creation? Or because it has not yet been tarnished by experience or smothered by unthinking adults? Why does this spirit, so vigorous in infancy, seem gradually to diminish as the child matures?

In a classic poem, William Wordsworth described how his own spirit gradually receded. The poem reads in part:

> *Heaven lies about us in our infancy!*
> *Shades of the prison-house begin to close*
> *Upon the growing Boy,*
> *But he beholds the light, and whence it flows,*
> *He sees it in his joy;*
> *The Youth, who daily farther from the east*
> *Must travel, still is Nature's Priest,*
> *And by the vision splendid*
> *Is on his way attended;*
> *At length the Man perceives it die away,*
> *And fade into the light of common day.*"[5]

Each child, I believe, has special spiritual gifts that may gradually diminish if they are not adequately nourished. When she picks up a worm, pulls apart a daisy or chases a butterfly, a child is showing us little miracles of life that we have long since taken for granted. As Jean Grasso Fitzpatrick writes, "The greatest challenge we all face as spiritual nurturers is to become attuned to the young child's authentic spirituality, which — unlike our own — is still such an integrated part of life... Children's exuberant spirituality is reflected in everything they do...A child shows us the extraordinary in the ordinary."[6]

Our task as spiritual nurturers becomes easier when we realize that we do not have to instill spirituality in a child, we have only to protect it from being trampled and to nourish its natural growth.

---

[5] William Wordsworth, "Ode on Intimations of Immortality from Recollections of Early Childhood."

[6] Jean Grasso Fitzpatrick, p. 45.

Part Two

The Spiritually Aware
Adult

Chapter 6

NOURISHING THE SPIRIT OF
THE TEACHER

In order for the children in Montessori classes today to fulfill Maria Montessori's great desire to create a better world for the future, it is vital for them to be in the care of adults — both parents and teachers — who live day to day in spiritual awareness. Both Maria Montessori and Rudolf Steiner, founder of the Waldorf Schools, wrote extensively about how young children, with their whole beings, literally soak up everything in their environment including the behavior and attitudes of the principal caretakers. Montessori called this unique way of learning the *absorbent mind*. It is well known to all who have studied her philosophy.

Regarding this phenomena Rudolf Steiner has said, "In the first part of his life, before the change of teeth, the child is, so to say, altogether a sense organ...It is receptive to impressions from the environment. If something striking occurs near him — for example, a burst of anger, then the reflection thereof goes right through the child. It will affect even his blood circulation and digestive system.

"These matters pertain to the most important characteristics of early childhood, whereas what you tell a child, what you teach him, makes a comparatively much weaker impression. What you actually are, whether you are good and your kindness is manifested in your gestures, or angry and temperamental, which becomes exhibited through your manners, is the most essential thing of all for the child. He is the sense organ reacting to everything to which he is exposed."[1]

The best preparation for teaching, Maria Montessori emphasized many times, is a study of one's self. This may be the most profound advice that she gave to us about teacher training. Most Montessorians have heard it, but how many have actually undertaken a serious in-depth study of their own values, beliefs, strengths, weaknesses, habits and omissions? How many have tried to determine how their personal characteristics either inhibit or enhance their relationships with children?

Montessori maintains that aspiring teachers need a guide, or mentor, to help with this self-study. "We insist...that a teacher must prepare himself interiorly by systematically studying himself so that he can tear out his most deeply rooted defects, those in fact which impede his relations with children. In order to discover these subconscious failings, we have need of a special kind of instruction. We must see ourselves as another sees us. We must be willing to accept guidance if we wish to become effective teachers."[2]

Today the curriculum and schedule of Montessori training centers is determined by time restraints, finances and practicality. What was once a two year training course is now finished in one year or is often reduced to several weeks in two consecutive summers with one or two days per month of classes during an internship in the intervening school year. In even more extreme cases training is limited to a correspondence course followed by two or three weeks of practical experience with materials. Where is the time for the best preparation for teaching?

Montessori was not the first or the most recent advocate of pursuing self-knowledge. The words, "Know thyself" came to us from the ancient Greeks where they were inscribed over the entrance to the temple called the Delphic Oracle. Plato, too, advised us with the famous words from his Apologia, "The unexamined life is not worth living."

Abraham Maslow elaborates on this: "The best way for a person to discover what he ought to do is to find out who and what he is...because the path to wiser choices...is via the discovery of the nature of the particu-

---

[1] Rudolf Steiner, Lecture in Torquay, England, 1924.

[2] Maria Montessori, *The Secret of Childhood*, Fides Publishers, pp. 182-183.

lar person. The more he knows about his own nature, his deep wishes, his temperament, his constitution, what he seeks and yearns for and what really satisfies him, the more effortless become his value choices."[3]

The well-known psychoanalyst, Carl Jung, has advised, "If there is anything we wish to change in the child, we should first examine it and see whether it is not something that could better be changed in ourselves."[4]

J.G. Bennett echoes this advice: "Whether we have to deal with children as parents or as teachers, our task begins with ourselves; and there is very much more to be derived by children from what those in contact with them do to put their own house in order than what they attempt to do to put the child's house in order."[5]

How does a Montessori teacher or one aspiring to be a Montessori teacher undertake the journey of self-discovery? Perhaps one of the first truths to ponder is that we are all, as human beings, wounded in some way. We all have what Carl Jung referred to as our shadow side. Our shadow is a part of us that we don't like to recognize, that we don't want to show to other people but which, unfortunately, we often project onto others. For example, people who are careless in the way they keep their belongings, whose desks or bedrooms are always cluttered and messy, will very often sharply criticize others for this particular characteristic.[6]

In order to hide our shadow side from others, most of us wear an invisible mask. The mask is not our true self but is the way we want others to see us. Teachers often wear the mask of perfection, never wanting to admit a weakness to their students, when actually talking about their own flaws would make them more accessible. "Mistakes bring us closer and make us better friends," Montessori writes, "Fraternity is born more easily on the road of error than on that of perfection"[7]

The journey of self-discovery leads us behind the masks to our true center. Here we find who we really are. We see our uniqueness as a

---

[3] Abraham Maslow, The Farther Reaches of Human Nature, p.111.

[4] Carl G. Jung, *The Integration of the Personality*, p. 285.

[5] J. G. Bennett, et al, *Spiritual Hunger of the Modern Child*, p. 82.

[6] Carl G. Jung, *Man and His Symbols*, 1968, p. 177 ff.

[7] Maria Montessori, *The Absorbent Mind*, p. 249.

person, we see our strengths, our weaknesses, our likes and dislikes, our fears and hopes, our self-hatred or our self-love. In this center we may discover a profound aloneness and an intense longing for something outside ourselves that gives meaning to life — in short, our spiritual longing, so often smothered by material accumulations and concern for what others think of us.

It is from this center of ourselves that we must operate as teachers — a center steeped in humility and awe as we recognize and reverence the wonders of the universe, the patterns of nature and the gift of life.

It is time to give renewed attention to Montessori's words: "One who would become a teacher according to our system must examine himself...and rid his heart of pride and anger. He must learn how to humble himself and be clothed with charity."[8]

The wisdom of Montessori's advice to undertake a study of one's self is supported by many movements, books and articles that urge us to operate from our center. Implicit in the *Bhagavad-Gita*, one of the most authoritative texts in Hindu philosophical literature, is a conception of becoming fully human only when we are inner directed and becoming dehumanized when we obey the dictates of external conditions. It maintains that when we operate from our authentic center we do not act out of anger, hate, attachment or obedience to authority. The self acts freely, for one is in a state of inner fulfillment, equanimity and freedom.[9]

In discovering one's self, I believe, it is also very important to recall one's childhood. This does not mean simply remembering a series of events. It means to feel intensely the moods of one's childhood, the emotions, the fears, the excitement, the questions (Did anyone answer them?), even the colors and smells of that early environment. Throughout his life Rudolf Steiner actively remembered his early years. In his autobiography, there is a tremendously vivid picture of his childhood in Austria. When he guided teachers, we are told, he always had these memories close at hand.[10]

---

[8] Maria Montessori, *The Secret of Childhood*, Fides Publishers, p. 187.

[9] Dale T. Snauwaert, "The Educational Theory of the Bhagavad-Gita," *Holistic Education Review*, Spring, 1992, p. 51-57.

[10] Adam Bittleston, "The Taste of Reality — Dr. Rudolf Steiner and the Child," J.G. Bennett et al, p. 94.

When I was instructing future teachers at the University of Pittsburgh, the first thing I asked them to do was to write about their early school experiences, recalling which of their own teachers had made them comfortable, made learning exciting, inspired them or made a significant difference in their lives. Next they recalled teachers who had made them afraid to participate or hesitant to try something new. The papers they wrote were more effective than anything I could tell them about relating to children. They were surprised to realize that even as children they had recognized that some teachers didn't really care about them, or simply operated on the surface, while others were committed from their hearts.

Such memories are helpful to the Montessori teacher who wishes to nourish the spirits of the children in her classroom. Spiritual nourishment can never be reduced to a set of techniques or a routine curriculum. It can only flow from the teacher's inner self. As the Jewish educator, A.I. Polack wrote "If you are to produce the ideal society of the future, the society in which children can thrive and express their personality in the atmosphere of shalom — which means not only peace but human welfare — those who are its architects and creators must be 'taught of the Lord': that is, spiritually minded people."[11]

This does not mean either that teachers must belong to an organized religion or that they must not belong to one. It means that whether or not they adhere to a particular creed, they must have a sense of the transcendent — a sense that there is something more to life than what they perceive with their senses. They must be able very honestly to honor the big questions of the universe, not by trying to give definitive answers but by acknowledging humbly that there are many aspects of life we cannot understand, even while we keep trying to explore.

Carolyn R. O'Grady, Assistant Professor of Education at Whitman College in Walla Walla, Washington, writes, "It is not essential to believe in a god to be spiritual, but it is important to believe in something that the word God has historically signified. It has been called by a myriad of names — Allah, Tao, Goddess, the sacred, immanence, community, the

---

[11] A. I. Polack, "Children Taught of the Lord," J. G. Bennett et al, p. 111.

ground of all being — and indicates an overarching reality, a oneness of all things. Whatever functions as the centering, unifying *linchpin* of our pattern of meaning functions as God for us. What is crucial is that an individual believes that there is a unifying force to creation and acts in the world based on that sense of unity."[12]

In my many years of experience I have met some very special Montessori teachers who have in one way or another discovered their innermost core. Each one seems to have about them a peacefulness and personal strength that comes, I believe, from operating out of his or her own true center. The teachers I am thinking about come from a variety of religious backgrounds but their spiritual natures that are reflected in their classrooms and in their conversations with children are remarkably similar. They reflect humility, sensitivity, responsiveness and a deep respect for nature and for all people.

To achieve the self-knowledge that underlies such spirituality, Montessori tells us, "requires help and instruction." Such help can be found in books, at workshops, at retreats and, as mentioned earlier, in guidance from a mentor or spiritual coach. Could this guidance be a permanent fixture of Montessori training and post-training professional development programs?

Certainly this aspect of teacher training is as important as the segments on math, language and cultural subjects. I would like to encourage each trainee and teacher to keep a spiritual journal; not an album that would have to be examined and graded, but a diary with a two-fold purpose. First, this diary could record the individual's spiritual journey. Secondly, it could be a storehouse of ideas for nurturing the spiritual growth of children in the classroom, including notations of appropriate children's books, songs, activities etc. that will support this important aspect of his or her work. It is time to give the spiritual nurturing of both teacher and children the priority it deserves in Montessori training programs. Without it we are neglecting what our founder insisted was the best preparation for teaching.

---

[12] Carolyn O'Grady, "Gathering Inspiration: Spirituality, Multicultural Education and Social Change," *Holistic Education Review*, Summer, 1994, p. 59.

Chapter 7

SUPPORT FOR DEEPENING SPIRITUALITY

As I am writing this book in the mid 1990's, I can sense a revival of interest in spirituality in many aspects of American culture. These are, for example, shelves full of books in conventional bookstores about angels. Two major Broadway productions had Angels in their titles — *Angels in America* and *City of Angels* — and a popular movie was *Angels in the Outfield*. A few years earlier the movie, *Gandhi*, about the great proponent of non-violence, surpassed all expectations. And films that go beyond everyday reality, such as *Star Wars* and *E.T.* soared at the box office.

A look at the paperback Best Seller Lists shows *Care of the Soul* and *Soul Mates* both by Thomas Moore and *The Road Less Traveled* by M. Scott Peck (over 600 weeks on the List). Among the hardback Best Sellers are the novel, *The Celestine Prophecy*, by James Redfield, *The Book of Virtues* by William J. Bennett, *The Seven Spiritual Laws of Success* by Deepak Chopra, *A History of God* by Karen Armstrong and *God, A Biography* by Jack Miles.

There is a significant renewal of interest in religious music, particularly Gregorian chant. Western religious leaders are studying Eastern philosophy and meditation in an effort to combine the best of both worlds. The works of the late Joseph Campbell is quite influential in a revival of interest in myth and words like *Zen*, *Sufi* and *Tao* have entered the everyday vocabulary of spiritual seekers in America. Christians have rediscovered the manuscripts of ancient and medieval mystics e.g. *The*

Cloud of the Unknowing and the writings of Meister Eckhart, Julian of Norwich and Hildegard of Bingen. Many people today are affirming the wisdom of the Jewish philosopher Martin Buber whose definitive work *I and Thou* showed the sacredness of relationships.

There is new interest these days in the spirituality of Native Americans and in the writings of the Dalai Lama, Thich Nhat Hanh and Krishnamurti. Interest in the ancient science of astrological guidance is extremely strong and the appeal of crystals, Tarot cards, drumming, channeling, para-psychology etc. is growing rapidly.

I am not proclaiming the merits of all the above. My point is simply that amid all our materialism in America, very noticeable attention is currently focused on spiritual phenomena.

Also flourishing are many techniques — both time-honored and modern — for self-understanding, relaxation, meditation and controlled movement. I feel that teachers can draw strength from some of these exercises as well as from examining spirituality in other methods of education. The following may be particularly helpful.

MINDFULNESS

This practice helps us to be in touch with life in the present moment by periodically stopping our random thoughts and giving full attention to what we are doing at that instant, whether it is taking deep breaths, walking, eating or washing dishes.

Mindful breathing is a particularly calming technique that helps us to recover ourselves completely and to encounter life in the present moment. Thich Nhat Hanh says, "As you breathe in, say to yourself, 'Breathing in, I know I am breathing in.' And as you breathe out say, 'Breathing out, I know I am breathing out.'...As you practice, your breath will become peaceful and gentle, and your mind and body will also become peaceful and gentle...In just a few minutes you can realize that fruit of meditation."[1] A chime clock or a bell that rings at regular intervals can prompt you to take three or four mindful breaths. Conscious breathing reminds us that we are alive - that we are enjoying the wonderful gift of life.

---

[1] Thich Nhat Hanh, Peace Is Every Step, pp. 8-9.

MEDITATION

This is a very private spiritual exercise consisting of deep prolonged focusing on a particular word or theme. There have been many different routines for meditation in various cultures and religions throughout the ages.

Transcendental Meditation is an easily learned technique that clears one's mind of the usual racing thoughts. The meditator sits in a relaxed position with eyes closed and mentally repeats a mantra — typically a meaningless word — for one or two 20 minute periods per day. This exercise usually induces relaxation, mental clarity and a centeredness that continues for hours beyond the actual period of meditation.

In some schools the staff meditates together before the children arrive. Nina Brown, director of the Hollow Reed School, writes, "When we meet to meditate each morning our purpose is to relax, to center ourselves and to draw on our inner resources to meet the day in our most positive way."[2] It also brings about a feeling of unity and connection among staff members.

Carolyn O'Grady in her article mentioned earlier, says "I am also a meditator... It is through meditation that I find the resources to persevere even when the task seems monumental."[3]

Religious meditation is particularly appropriate for people of faith who use a religious word or phrase as a mantra when meditating. Another form of religious meditations is silently focusing on a sacred theme or scriptural passage for a prolonged length of time.

CONTROLLED MOVEMENT

In the Montessori classroom children learn control of movement when doing the Practical Life Exercises and Walking on the Line. Teachers, too, can reap benefits from exercising this kind of control.

Yoga is an ancient practice of uniting soul and body in a series of postures that lead to relaxation by physically stretching the body and limbs and extending the power of concentration. Not only does Yoga provide a

---

[2] Nina Brown, "Supporting the Spiritual Aspect in Children," *Holistic Education Review*, Summer, 1989, p. 41.

[3] Carolyn O' Grady in *Holistic Education Review*, Summer, 1994, p. 57.

very practical approach to attaining a high level of physical fitness, it also helps to stabilize the emotions and to elevate one's mental attitude.

T'ai Chi also known as T'ai Chi Ch'uan, is a series of slow dance-like movements sequentially performed in a very slow motion. The movements are designed to synchronize and align the mind and body with flowing motions demanding constant concentration, relaxed posture and slow, even breathing. T'ai Chi facilitates the flow of energy in the body.

Ross Sidwell of the State University of New York writes, "I have taught the 8-10 minute seventy movement form of T'ai Chi... to undergraduate and graduate students in education classes ...Many report a growing awareness...of *their* mind and body...A mind/body reconnection in the individual...is the first and necessary step towards the creation of a spiritual dimension in education — one which ultimately connects the centered individual to the universe."[4]

SELF-UNDERSTANDING

In an article entitled "Where to Start in the Spiritual Life," philosopher writer, Robert Powell, states "The word *spiritual* is difficult to define because our ordinary experience does not touch it... The nearest indication of its meaning is to say that it begins with self-knowing, with being aware of one's thoughts, desires, fears, motivations; in short, the whole machinery of the mind."[5]

There are many tests, books, exercises and systems designed to help individuals to understand themselves. Such resources are constantly being appended or replaced by newer strategies. Some that currently offer significant aid in self understanding are described here briefly.

Myers-Briggs Type Indicator, described in the book, *Gifts Differing*,[6] is a very popular instrument (similar to a questionnaire) that reveals individual differences and leads to an appreciation of these differences. It points out a person's strengths and how these strengths can be used effectively especially when selecting a career, experiencing problems or

---

[4] Ross Sidwell, "Only Connect: T'ai Chi and a Spiritual Dimension of Teacher Preparation," Holistic Education Review, Summer 1989, p. 58-61

[5] *The Inner Directions Journal*, Winter, 1995, p. 8.

[6] Isabel Briggs Myers with Peter B. Myers, *Gifts Differing*.

making significant changes. A simple form of the Myers-Briggs Inventory can be self-administered and self-assessed. A more detailed Inventory can be administered and interpreted by a mental health professional.

The Enneagram is a very old typology that can be helpful to people seeking self-knowledge and spiritual guidance. This self-administered assessment claims there are nine different types of people defined by their needs: 1. To Be Perfect; 2. To Be Needed; 3. To Succeed; 4. To Be Special; 5. To Perceive; 6. To Be Secure; 7. To Avoid Pain; 8. To Be Against; 9. To Avoid.

Like any other typology the Enneagram downplays the uniqueness of individuals by assigning them to a category. However, the discovery of regular patterns of behavior in one's self or others can be a helpful source of self-knowledge and an aid to understanding those with whom one shares a family or working relationship. The Enneagram typology reveals not only a person's type but also offers means to modify that determinacy with the possibility of meaningful change.[7]

Transactional Analysis is a method that helps one to recognize and evaluate how he or she interacts with others. Formulated by the psychiatrist Eric Berne and popularized in such books as *I'm OK, You're OK*[8], and *Born to Win*[9], this system helps individuals to become aware of their remarks to others and to categorize them as parent statements, child statements or adult statements. Such awareness helps one to see the pitfalls of speaking as a child or parent to other adults and the wisdom of operating in the adult mode.

RELIGIOUS ROOTS

Many of today's adults were nurtured in a particular religious faith during their early years. For some this faith is still very meaningful today and provides a strong center and inspiration for their lives. Other adults have all but dropped the religion of their childhood.

It is helpful, I believe, for teachers trying to come to know their true selves to take time to reflect deeply on their own religious roots, whether

---

[7] Richard Rohr and Andreas Ebert, *Discovering the Enneagram*, p. 22.

[8] Thomas Harris, *I'm OK, You're OK; A Practical Guide to Transactional Analysis.*

[9] Muriel James and Dorothy Jongeward, *Born to Win.*

or not they are still affiliated with that particular faith. Was your religious training age-appropriate at the time you received it? Can you think of incidents when it gave you comfort? When it gave you strength to do something difficult? When it helped you to be honest, truthful, kind or self-sacrificing? When the liturgy or services gave you a sense of peace, transcendence or a calling to a meaningful mission? Perhaps your childhood religion had little or no influence in your life. Or perhaps it had more influence than you ever realized. What energy can you draw from it now for your personal spiritual journey? Does it still influence your daily routine in any way?

One Montessori teacher related to me that in this type of reflection she had actually experienced a conversion. Not a conversion from one religion to another, but a conversion from the superficiality of her present religious affiliation to the actual spiritual treasures in its own scriptural origins.

HOLISTIC EDUCATION

In addition to help for their personal spiritual development, Montessorians can profit by becoming familiar with other educational movements that are concerned with spirituality. The magazine *Holistic Education Review*, from which some of the previous quotations were drawn, is the organ of a vibrant and coherent movement called Holistic Education that emerged in the United States in the 1980's. The purpose of this movement is not to reform or restructure education but to work for a fundamental transformation. The holistic paradigm is not new. According to its founders, it has its roots in the nineteenth century educational theories of Jean Jacques Rousseau, Johann Pestalozzi and Freidrich Froebel who all emphasized the spiritual nature of the human being. In their developing effort the current holistic leaders draw heavily on the work of Maria Montessori and Rudolf Steiner. Despite differences in terminology, emphasis and educational technique, these educators asserted that the developing person unfolds from within, guided by an internal creative source. For them, education meant what its Latin root suggests: a leading out or drawing forth of life energies and personal potentials that exist within the individual.

The purpose of education, according to the holistic thinkers, is to nourish the growth of every person's intellectual, emotional, social, physical, artistic and spiritual potentials. It does not focus on determining which facts or skills adults should teach children, but on creating a learning community that will stimulate the growing person's creative and inquisitive engagement with the world.[10]

WALDORF EDUCATION

Holistic Education also incorporates much of the work of Rudolf Steiner who formulated the educational principles that spawned the Waldorf Schools. Steiner (1861-1925) was born nine years before Montessori's birth in 1870 and died 27 years before her death in 1952. Both were Europeans, neither one was trained as a teacher, but they both brought new vision to education that challenged the embedded academic practices of the early twentieth century.

Rudolf Steiner was an Austrian philosopher, scientist and artist. He developed a science of the spirit that he called *anthroposophy*, "a way of knowledge which would lead the spiritual in the human being to the spiritual in the universe."

At the request of Emil Molt, an industrialist who was General Director of the Waldorf Astoria Cigarette Company, Rudolf Steiner founded the first Waldorf School in Stuttgart, Germany, in 1919. This was just twelve years after Maria Montessori had started her Casa dei Bambini in Rome. Like Montessori, Steiner had many followers; Waldorf schools spread in Europe and to the United States.

For many years professional educators have emphasized the differences between Waldorf schools and Montessori schools without acknowledging their commonalties. For example, Montessori introduces the academic subjects — math, language arts and geography — in the class for three to six year olds. Steiner offered no academics, not even any children's books in the classroom, until children were seven. In the years prior to that he cultivated their imagination with art, music, drama and especially by telling stories. Montessori reserved imaginative activities and myths until the elementary years. Although their methods differed, both these

---

[10] Summarized from "Philosophical Foundations" by Ron Miller; Carol L. Flake, (ed.), *Holistic Education: Principles, Perspectives and Practices*, pp. 78-80.

visionaries placed heavy emphasis on the first seven years of life as having profound significance for the child's later emotional and spiritual development.

Both Maria Montessori and Rudolph Steiner had several of their books published by the Theosophical Society in Adyar, India. Steiner, in fact, was a member of this society in Germany until he formed his own system of anthroposophy. Montessori's connection with the Theosophical Society was in her later life when its members invited her to give a teacher training course on the grounds of their headquarters in Adyar in 1939. In her biography of Maria Montessori, Rita Kramer states, "Montessori and the Theosophists had always found each other's thinking congenial. [A] core of Theosophy was the principle of self-realization leading to the liberation of the true self and to ultimate wisdom. There was some affinity between these beliefs and Montessori's view of education as a process of liberating the spirit of the child."[11]

Of particular interest to our subject at hand is the two-year Waldorf teacher training course. The entire first year of this program is devoted to self-development during which most participants experience a fundamental change in themselves as they discover their true centers, explore personal characteristics that will influence their teaching and experience solitude, music, art and some of the great treasures of literature.

QUAKER EDUCATION

Quaker education, as carried out in schools operated by the Society of Friends, also has deep spiritual roots that go back to its founder, George Fox, in 17th century England. Fox believed that "there is that of God in everyone." Quakers speak of this as the *Seed* of the divine within every human soul — a seed that must be nourished with particular disciplines of the spiritual life. Many Quaker schools hold regular meetings for silence where students listen to their own inner voices.

Although recognized as academically strong, these Schools tend not to emphasize particular techniques so much as the Quaker *vision* of the human spirit. Their schools affirm the worth of every student and offer

---

[11] Rita Kramer, *Maria Montessori*, A Biography, pp. 342-343.

each student age-appropriate opportunities to participate in service projects that help others in the school and the surrounding community.

Perhaps because of this great emphasis on the divine seed within every human person, adult Quakers are often at the forefront of movements for peace, for reform of criminal punishment and for bringing justice and respect to minority groups, particularly Native Americans, African-Americans and women. In other words, the education of many Friends students comes to fruition in adult leadership of various humanitarian efforts that help to make a better world.

In the preceding descriptions I do not mean to imply that every Waldorf or Quaker school is a perfect example of spiritual nurture. Perfection does not exist in everyday reality. But these schools, as well as others incorporating holistic education, share the goal of Montessori to nurture the spirit of each child. Investigation of their literature and visits to their schools can offer Montessorians a valuable cross-fertilization of spiritual ideals.

Maria Montessori, Rudolf Steiner, George Fox and other holistic thinkers all view their educational work as part of a larger transformation of modern Western culture — an effort to take us from overwhelming materialism to spiritual values, and from competition and conflict to personal and global peace. We can accomplish this only by rising above our differences and realizing that the inherent basic truth of the spiritual nature of the child is larger than any single perspective or methodology.

Chapter 8

COMMUNITY FOR TEACHERS

The journey to wholeness cannot be made alone. By nature we are social beings and our spiritual journeys are nearly always made in some kind of relationship with others — with our families, our co-workers, a special friend or perhaps in a small intimate group. One of the most effective means of nurturing the spirituality of teachers is a strong sense of community in the staff.

What do we mean by the term *community*? I like to think of community as a group of people who come together for a common purpose in a spirit of helpfulness and harmony. But this, or perhaps any other description, fails to reveal its spiritual essence. Community must be experienced rather than defined. Scott Peck tells us that "there is no adequate one sentence definition [for community]. Like electricity...it is inherently mysterious, miraculous, unfathomable...It is a realm where words are never fully suitable and language itself falls short."[1]

In his book about communities, Dick Westley parallels this thought: "Community is much more than a social reality, something humans can achieve by their will and their efforts. It is, rather, one of the most profound and important of the *spiritual* realities. As something 'of the spirit,' it is also something of a mystery, more easily experienced than talked about."[2]

---

[1] M. Scott Peck, A Different Drum, p. 60.

[2] Dick Westley, *Good Things Happen*, p. 24.

Although it is difficult to define, there are certain attributes that we can recognize in a genuine community. By its very nature, community is inclusive rather than exclusive. A staff community cannot exclude a teacher who appears to be intolerant of others or who monopolizes the conversation. That person must first feel welcomed simply as he or she is. This acceptance, itself, may help the person, over time, to change inappropriate habits and attitudes.

As an inclusive group a community appreciates the differences in its members. This does not mean that the members agree on everything. But differences are neither dismissed nor allowed to lead to alienation. They are recognized and respected as the realities of society. Commitment to the integrity of the community is especially important when serious differences arise.

I believe that it is possible for the staff in a Montessori school to function as a community of support for each other and that this experience can nourish each one's personal spiritual journey. Achieving real community, however, is not easy. It will not simply come into being when the board or head of school announces, "We are going to form a staff community." Communities don't just happen; we build them as we build relationships. They can take shape only gradually, even obliquely, in an atmosphere of respect, openness and trust in each other's spiritual integrity.

Carole Cooper and Julie Boyd, founders of Global Learning Communities with headquarters in Australia, bemoan the fact that most teachers function in isolation rather than in cooperation. "The adult in the next classroom is not someone they confide in about matters of teaching practice because it is too threatening. There is not time for teachers to collaborate even if they want to. In most schools teachers do not see each other teach; they do not know each others' disciplines. Therefore it is difficult for them to even imagine the far reaching possibilities of collaboration."[3]

Currently worldwide there is a movement toward transformational education that is dedicated to changing the situation where each teacher

[3] Newsletter of Global Learning Communities, 163 George Street, Launceston, Tasmania, 7250, Australia.

closes her door, guards her territory and never admits to having a problem. "Trying always to project an image of total strength and competence," Dick Westley writes, "exacts a heavy psychological toll on the individual and makes authentic community impossible...Community has something to do with being open enough to share weakness, to accept one's vulnerability and finitude not only in the secret recesses of one's heart, but also in the presence of others. Paradoxically that's where the real power of community comes from."[4]

Admitting one's weaknesses is difficult and there are some who cannot imagine ever doing so. However, if a person, perhaps after months of groping for courage, is finally able to give voice to his or her most vulnerable part, there is nearly always an immediate feeling of relief and a sense of receiving support from those who have listened. Because we are all flawed in one way or another, the sharing of weakness helps us to form strong human bonds.

But community is not only about sharing weaknesses. Community breeds helpfulness, strength, intimacy and a special kind of shared laughter that comes from knowing each other well and looking at situations from the same perspective. "If we are going to use the word [community] in a meaningful way," Scott Peck writes, "we must restrict it to a group of individuals who have learned how to communicate honestly with each other, whose relationships go deeper than their masks of composure, and who have developed some significant commitment to rejoice together, mourn together, to delight in each other and make [each] others' conditions [their] own."[5]

No community can exist without open communication. Each person must feel that the community is a "safe place" to express feelings and concerns without the threat of retaliation. "I" statements are appropriate; derogatory statements are not acceptable. For example one can say, "I feel that I am asked to do more than my share," rather than "You never do your part."

I believe that community among the staff is a prerequisite to all other forms of community that are desirable in a Montessori school, such as

---

[4] Dick, Westley, p. viii.

[5] M. Scott Peck, *A Different Drum*, p. 59.

community among the children in a classroom or envisioning the whole school as a community of families. Staff community may be the most difficult to achieve but the one that will yield the greatest good for the school. How then does one go about helping a group of professional teachers to let go of competition and individual success in order to enter into a spirit of mutual helpfulness in a community of peers? The answer is gently, gently, gently. Parker Palmer says that "community is another one of those strange things that elude us if we aim directly at it...[It] comes as a by-product of commitment and struggle. It comes when we step forward to right some wrong, to heal some hurt, to give some service. Then we discover each other as allies in resisting the diminishments of life."[6]

I am personally aware of a Montessori school where the teachers for many years closely guarded their own territories. There was little or no sharing of materials or ideas for staff development. During one year, because of state regulations, the whole staff had to take two difficult education courses while they were teaching full time. The burden was great, so out of necessity they began sharing it—lending each other books, doing research together, taking turns going to the library for everyone's books, critiquing each other's papers and studying together for exams.

When preparing to open school the following September there was a noticeably different sense of unity among the staff. They got together to make new language materials and a once unheard of offer was now frequently heard, "I'm going to K-Mart. Does anyone need anything?" Community was beginning to form, not because these teachers had decided to form it, but because they had shared a burden together.

Other experiences that have helped teachers to build community are: going together to an Outward Bound program where each person must trust a colleague who is holding the ropes while he or she attempts a challenging feat; attending a community building workshop such as those sponsored by GATE — the Global Alliance For Transforming Education;[7] working together to solve a particular problem that seriously affects the school; holding a staff retreat; taking part in discussions of

---

[6] Parker J. Palmer, *A Place Called Community*, p. 18.

[7] GATE, P. O. Box 21, Grafton, VT, 05146.

perceptive questions, such as "What does education really mean?" "How does spirituality differ from religion?"

Susan Swift, head of The Children's House and Montessori School of Northampton, MA held a weekend retreat for her staff of nine at a home available to them on a lake in Maine. "In May of that year," Susan said, "the whole staff was feeling fragmented. It had been the first year of our elementary program and that teacher, particularly, was feeling isolated. We decided to get everyone together, without spouses or children, for some walks, canoeing, cooking together and sitting around in the evening — just letting each one say how she/he felt the year had gone. By withdrawing from our 'too busy' routine, we felt we became human again — sharing ideas and a lot of laughs. We're going to do it again in January."

In most schools there is little or no time for such a community building effort. Teachers can work side by side, day after day, and never know each other as human beings. I believe that setting aside time and some funds for a simple staff retreat, particularly before the school year starts, may be one of the best investments a school board or school owner can make. Very likely it will pay year-long dividends in human understanding, caring, helpfulness and positive attitudes.

Teachers who can most readily take part in a staff community are usually those who have experienced community previously in another setting, such as in their teacher training. Institutions that are dedicated to transformational education such as Southwestern College in Santa Fe[8] or the Naropa Institute in Boulder[9] focus on the inner preparation of the teacher and meaningful participation in a learning community. They emphasize that "Where the heart is opened and nurtured in teacher training, there is the possibility of connecting with the best in our children."[10]

The programs and workshops offered at these centers are in harmony with Maria Montessori's emphasis on spirituality and with her insistence that teachers root out any characteristics that impede their relationships with children. A supportive community can continue to help teachers on this journey to wholeness.

[8] Southwestern College, P.O. Box 4788 Sante Fe, NM, 87502-4788.

[9] Naropa Institute, 2130 Arapahoe Ave., Boulder, CO, 80302-9926.

[10] Richard C. Brown, "Buddhist-Inspired Early Childhood Education at the Naropa Institute," *Holistic Education Review*, Winter, 1991, p.16.

Part Three

Ideas For Children
in
Non-Sectarian Settings

Chapter 9

CULTIVATING STILLNESS

*The method in the Children's Houses prepares
the children in the daily life of the classroom
by exercises which are, in themselves, quite
independent of religious education, but which
seem to be a preparation for it. In fact, they
aid in perfecting the child, in making him calm,
obedient, attentive to his own movements, capable
of silence and recollection.*

- Maria Montessori[1]

A very important step in nurturing either one's own spirit or a child's spirit, is to prepare an environment where stillness can be cultivated with some regular frequency. It is almost impossible for one's spirit to thrive in the constant din and hubbub of daily life. Some special places and special times must be set aside for quiet — for one to be open to one's inner voice. "Silence," says Montessori, "often brings us the knowledge which we had not fully realized, that we possess within ourselves an interior life. The child by means of silence sometimes becomes aware of this for the first time."[2]

---

[1] E. M. Standing, Editor, *The Child in the Church*, p.24

[2] E. M. Standing, *Maria Montessori, Her Life and Work*, p.226.

In the world of children today there is very little, if any, quiet time. In most homes the TV plays constantly, and where the TV is not available, such as in the car, the sounds of the radio or audio tapes fill the air. Add to this the noises of traffic, telephones, lawn mowers, dishwashers, mixers, vacuum cleaners, computers that beep and buzz, video games that bang and squawk, children's fire engines that blare and battery operated toys that pelt us with all kinds of invasive sounds.

Because uninterrupted noise has become so commonplace in American life, many of today's children have never known the tranquility of silence. This does not mean that children do not like quiet and stillness. It simply means that they have not had an opportunity to relish it.

I believe that children, when they have a chance, naturally seek out spaces and moments of quiet to be alone with their own thoughts. Many biographies and autobiographies of significant people include descriptions of special places where, as children, they could wallow in privacy and let imagination run free.

In her autobiography, the writer, Annie Dillard, tells of the special attic bedroom where she loved to spend time alone drawing pictures of her baseball mitt and sorting her rock collection. That room, she writes, "interested me especially for a totemic brown water stain on a sloping plaster wall. The stain looked like a square-rigged ship heeled over in a storm. I examined this ship for many months...it had no lines, only forms awash, which rose faintly from the plaster and deepened slowly and dramatically as I watched and the seas climbed and the wind rose before anyone could furl the sails. Those distant dashes over the water—were they men sliding overboard?"[3]

The late poet, Phyllis McGinley, wrote of a cupola in the old Victorian house of her Aunt Jeanette, whom she visited during several summers. "An eccentric, spiraling set of stairs led up to it from the second floor...it was sweetly, entirely, irresistibly private. No eyes peering in on me, no household voice reached me once I closed the door. I could look out over the treetops and imagine myself anything from Rapunzel to the Little Lame Prince."[4]

---

[3] Annie Dillard, *An American Childhood*, p.126.

[4] Phyllis McGinley, "Privacy," *House and Garden*, January, 1957.

Boys, too, tell of huts, tree houses or special spaces in the woods where they could be alone with their thoughts. In *The Education of Little Tree*, the young Cherokee boy describes his hideaway: "Following the spring branch [of the river] was how I found my secret place. It was a little ways up the side of the mountain and hemmed in with laurel. It was not very big, a grass knoll with an old sweet gum tree bending down. When I saw it I knew it was my secret place, and so I went there a whole lot.

"Ol' Maud [his dog] taken to going with me. She liked it too, and we would sit under the sweet gum and listen — and watch. Ol' Maud never made a sound in the secret place. She knew it was a secret."[5]

Special places for quiet are equally as important for adults. The late Joseph Campbell, a renowned expert on myth, emphasized this in an interview when Bill Moyers asked him, "What does it mean to have a sacred place?" Campbell replied: "This is an absolute necessity for anybody today. You must have a room, or a certain hour or so a day, where you don't know what was in the newspapers that morning, you don't know who your friends are, you don't know what you owe anybody, you don't know what anybody owes to you. This is a place where you can simply experience and bring forth what you are and what you might be. This is the place of creative incubation."[6]

Madeleine L'Engle, the very imaginative writer of books for children and adults, describes where she goes to regain her sense of proportion when she is frustrated. "My special place is a small brook in a green glade, a circle of quiet from which there is no visible sign of human beings. There's a natural stone bridge over the brook, and I sit there, dangling my legs and looking through the foliage at the sky reflected in the water... and I move slowly into a kind of peace that is marvelous."[7]

In *Care of The Soul*, Thomas Moore emphasizes the need for regular retreat from the world, no matter how simple or brief it may have to be. He tells about Carl Jung who built a stone tower that "became a sacred place for his soul work where he could paint on the walls, write his dreams, think his thoughts, enjoy his memories and record his visions."

[5] Forrest, Carter, *The Education of the Little Tree*, p. 58.

[6] Joseph Campbell with Bill Moyers, *The Power of Myth*, p. 92.

[7] Madeleine L'Engle, *A Circle of Quiet*, p.4.

While most of us today cannot build a tower, we can dedicate a room, even a closet or a corner of the house or garden for giving time to our spirit. It could be as simple as keeping a spiritual journal or having a drawer or a box where dreams and thoughts are treasured. "It might be the decision to take a walk through the woods instead of touring the shopping mall. It might be keeping the television set in a closet so that watching it becomes a special occasion. It could be the purchase of a piece of sacred art that helps focus attention on spirituality...

Spirituality need not be grandiose...but it asks for some small measure of withdrawal from a world set up to ignore the soul."[8]

How then can we, as Montessori teachers, ensure that some time and space is set aside in our daily routines to give children a taste of spirit-nourishing stillness?

THE GROUP SILENCE GAME

Maria Montessori played an interesting role in the history of classroom silence. Actually she liberated children from the harsh silence forced upon them in the old traditional classrooms. Realizing that young children were in the critical period for language development, Montessori permitted them to speak freely, but respectfully, in the classroom. Rather than enforcing silence, she presented silence as a special challenge — something to be achieved. To give the children this challenge she devised the Silence Game — a group exercise that is still used in some, but not all, Montessori classrooms today.

To begin the exercise, the teacher displays a signal that has been already introduced to the children, such as a large card with the word *SILENCE* on it. As each child notices the signal he or she stops working, keeps silent and sits perfectly still, trying not to move a muscle. A calm quiet gradually extends itself throughout the room and children hear the usually unnoticed sounds of the clock ticking or the refrigerator humming. After a few minutes of perfect silence, the teacher calls one child's name in a barely audible whisper. That child rises slowly and tiptoes to where the teacher is standing, proceeding so quietly that no one else will hear her moving. This continues until all the children have been called.

---

[8] Thomas Moore, *Care of the Soul*, pp. 208-11.

Then the *SILENCE* card is taken down and the children return to their individual activities.

In his biography of Maria Montessori, E.M. Standing tells of a directress who asked the children to say what they had heard in the silence. Besides the usual sounds of a chair creaking and a train chugging in the distance, "one child said she heard 'the Spring coming' and another 'the voice of God speaking inside me.'"[9]

The Silence Game should never be used to try to calm children when they are loud and unruly. Rather, it is to be presented when they are working well to show them that they can extend their self control to an even greater degree. Together, with everyone's cooperation, they have the power to create silence.

"Maria Montessori placed the Silence Lesson as an extremely significant element in her schools," Sofia Cavalletti writes. "The silence...arises very slowly, through the control of even the slightest movement, and extends to enfold the whole group of children in some way... Therefore it should not be asked of the children when we sense they are not disposed toward it; silence is not an aid for the teacher to bring the class to order; it is a help to the meditative spirit of the child."[10]

The Silence Game lets children experience the peace of stillness. It also teaches them that silence is not automatic in our lives; we have to make an effort to attain it. At home this may mean turning off the TV or radio at certain times during the day or week or setting aside a special area that is not reached by the usual noises.

INDIVIDUAL SILENCE GAME

Joan Gilbert, a Montessori teacher at Penn-Mont Academy, Altoona, PA, extended the experience of this exercise by designing an individual Silence Game that could be practiced more frequently. She writes, "This variation of the Silence Game enables an individual child to choose to be silent and motionless at any time during class. Maintaining this individual silence is more difficult than group silence because other children in the class continue their normal activity."

[9] E. M. Standing, *Maria Montessori, Her Life and Work*, p. 226.

[10] Sofia Cavaletti, *The Religious Potential of the Child*, p. 36.

The materials for individual silence are a special small rug, significantly different from all the other small rugs in the classroom, and a basket containing a card with the word *Silence* and an hourglass (one or three minute timer). The timer provides a definite beginning and closure, enabling the child to be independent.

For this exercise Joan permits an exception to the usual procedure of children placing their working materials *on* a small rug and sitting or kneeling *beside* this rug to do the work. When practicing individual silence, she feels, the actual work takes place within the child. So anyone doing this exercise can remove his shoes and sit on the special rug with the silence card in front of him. While the timer is running, the child remains silent and motionless. This is an uninterruptible exercise. Other children are asked not to speak to, bump against or disturb in any other way the child who has chosen to do individual silence.

Joan comments, "Because I expected that the five and six year-olds would be the ones most frequently drawn to it, I was very surprised to see how popular it was with all the children, particularly the youngest, who often have the hardest time maintaining stillness in the group Silence Game. It's somehow impressive to see such little ones choose silence as their work, while all the children around them are busy with other activities."

POSITION CARDS

Another variation of silence and stillness that Joan designed is the individual use of a set of Position Cards. Each card illustrates, with either a drawing or a photograph, a child standing or kneeling in a position that in a general way suggests reverence and care. Joan provides the possible meaning of the gestures, indicated here in parentheses, for the teachers. The child sees only the cards bearing illustrations that she is to imitate.

Some examples of these positions are: standing with arms crossed over the chest (the sign language symbol for love); standing with arms held as if cradling a baby (caring); standing with one hand extended as if holding something (giving); standing with both hands forming a cup (receiving).

Materials for this exercise are a small mat and a tray holding a one-minute timer and a set of cards. Again the child removes her shoes, stands

on the small mat, sets the timer and silently assumes the position illustrated on the top card. She holds perfectly still in this position for one
minute and then proceeds to the next card. The child is challenged to
notice the details of each position and to imitate it as closely as possible
while remaining silent. Afterwards Joan sometimes asks the child how
she felt when she was standing in one or two of the various positions.

THE QUIET CORNER

Some Montessori teachers set aside a small area of the classroom or
an alcove as a Quiet Corner, that is different from the traditional reading
corner. Joanne Alex of the Stillwater Montessori School in Old Town, ME,
has her Quiet Corner behind a large fish tank that is on a classroom shelf.
In this Quiet Corner there is a small table and chair where one child at a
time can sit and look at the fish, gaze out the window at the trees, examine a lovely plant or observe an object on the table such as a beautiful
seashell. The child does not speak while in the Quiet Corner; he simply
observes and appreciates a few of nature's wonders.

A SEASONAL QUIET CORNER

Another description of a Quiet Corner was given to me by Joyce
Frugé, a Montessori teacher in Detroit, MI., who says, "In our desire to do
for the children, we forget that sometimes they just need to be."

The need for a space where children could reflect was reinforced
for Joyce by the learning specialist and author, Dr. Jane Healy, who once
asked a well-known physicist if he remembered his early learning
experiences. He paused, and said, "My mother had a flour sifter in the
kitchen and every day after school I would get the flour and sit on the
floor and sift it."

"Were you learning measurement?" Dr. Healy asked eagerly. "No,
I was just sifting," the physicist replied.

The point was that in the process of sifting, he was also pondering.
"I love the word *ponder*," Joyce says. "That's what the Quiet Corner is all
about.

In Joyce's Quiet Corner one child at a time sits silently near a lovely
rug facing a section of the wall that has been painted pure white. This
plain background serves to accent the seasonal objects that Joyce places

on the rug. However, before placing the symbols in the Quiet Corner, Joyce introduces them to the children in a group activity.

"In spring our project is called New Life. "Each child plants his or her own seeds in a small container of soil and waters them. Within a few days, we have sprouts. As each child notices his seeds sprouting, he comes to me and says, "I found New Life."

"We also use New Life for a different version of the Silence Game. I put a sample of New Life, such as a glass butterfly or a small ceramic bird in a nest, in a special box. With a background of beautiful soft music, the object is removed, then one child at a time walks on the line reverently carrying the object while all the other children remain silent. When I whisper "stop" the child stands still, and silently hands the object to the child who is sitting in front of him. After several children have had a turn, the example of New Life is moved to the Quiet Corner."

Other symbols of New Life that Joyce uses in this way are an onion and a potato so children can ponder the miracle of sprouting, a real bird's nest that was once carefully prepared for the eggs that contained New Life, a selection of young plants, a book with beautiful pictures of Spring and a book with pictures of new babies. This "pondering" section changes frequently as each of these reminders are placed there, inviting the children to "come and see."

A seasonal Quiet Corner helps children to be aware of the cycles of life and to appreciate the miracles of nature that we so often take for granted. In the fall it features symbols of the harvest — apples, squash, pumpkins, corn. Children can feel thankful for our food that the harvest from the earth has given us.

A JAPANESE ROCK GARDEN ACTIVITY

Kassie Yarrison, a teacher at Our Children's Center Montessori School in State College, PA, designed a lovely rock garden project for individual quiet in her classroom.

"The Japanese Rock Garden activity came about while our three to six group was involved in a cultural study of Japan. Its aim is for the child to feel serenity and realize the reverence of the Japanese people for the beauty of nature. To introduce the work, we talked about gardens and their purpose of celebrating nature, and viewed pictures of Rock Gardens in Japan. The children heard that Japanese people visit the gardens quietly, not using the rocks for climbing as in our country. The viewing of the rocks and the sand is a meditative process; it is a peaceful place.

"Our activity was set up in this manner: A relatively quiet part of the room was chosen for a low table in front of which the children could kneel. On the table was a large tray (about 12" X 15") of sand, beside the table a basket held a bowl of beautiful rocks, a small spade and rake (about 6" long designed as tools for house plants) and a small brush and dustpan. Above the table we placed a photograph of a man raking the sand in a lovely rock garden. The children were instructed, "This is a work for one person. There are no watchers allowed. It is a good work to do when you want some quiet time to yourself."

"First, the child slowly and gently flattens the sand using the palm of the hand. Then the rocks are arranged as desired, some or all can be used. The sand is then carefully raked in a pleasing pattern; any spills are cleaned up. The rock arrangement can be left for others to admire (the option chosen by most children) or taken down.

"This activity produced remarkable results. Children and sand have a natural affinity, yet very few reminders were needed that this sand was not for digging. The children seemed very taken up with the arrangement of the rocks, often moving them about, always gently, until satisfied. Several children not often seen at activities requiring lengthy concentration seemed drawn to the Rock Garden. We felt what it must be like to actually be in a lovely, serene rock garden. Some activities are very special pleasures, when you see the results they produce — this was one such activity."

AN OUTDOOR QUIET SPACE

Another lovely idea is to reserve a small semi-secluded outdoor area with a bench where one person at a time can contemplate nature. A sign, perhaps carved in wood, can designate it as "The Quiet Space" or if flowers are growing there, "The Quiet Garden." It is wise to have this space within view of the playground so teachers supervising outdoor activities can give permission for a child to go alone to "The Quiet Space," and can keep an eye on that child while he or she is there.

A "Quiet Garden" could be designed by and cared for by elementary students. Several Montessori teachers have suggested planting sun-flowers and scarlet runner beans to climb on strings, bamboo poles or a trellis. They can form an archway that serves as an entrance to the Quiet Garden or they could form a little shelter over the bench that gives the area a natural feeling of serenity.

"Silence predisposes the soul for certain inner experiences," E.M. Standing tells us. "You are not the same after silence as you were before it...It is one of the tragedies of our mechanical age that so many people grow up without ever having discovered the beauty of silence."[11]

Standing wrote these words in the 1950's. Now forty years later, silence is even rarer in our culture, as new sources of noise are added daily to our lives. Because this continuous racket might be smothering the fledgling spirits of children, it seems more important than ever before to give them some experiences of stillness. How wonderful if opportunities for silence could have a new resurgence in Montessori environments!

---

[11] E.M. Standing, *Maria Montessori, Her Life and Work*, p.226-227.

Chapter 10

WONDER — THE LEAVEN OF SPIRITUALITY

Tell me, tell me everything!
What makes it Winter
And then Spring?
Which are the children
Butterflies?
Why do people keep
Winking their eyes?
Where do birds sleep?
Do bees like to sting?
Tell me, tell me please, everything!

Tell me, tell me, I want to know!
What makes leaves grow
In the shapes they grow?
Why do goldfish
Keep chewing? And rabbits
Warble their noses?
Just from habits?
Where does the wind
When it goes away go?
Tell me, or don't even grown-ups know?

Harry Behn[1]

How precious is the gift of wonder! In a child it is like a delicate seedling that one hopes will never be trampled on and never allowed to

---

[1] Kitty Clevenger, editor, *The Magic of Children*, unnumbered pages.

dry up. With careful nourishment childhood wonder will flower into a deep reverence for nature that can keep one's spirit alive into a vital old age. People with an active sense of wonder are rarely bored, no matter how young or old they are.

Basically, wonder is nourished by opportunities to observe the intricate workings of nature. Truly such observation is a spiritual act. Joseph Cornell, a pre-eminent nature educator, writes, "The unutterable beauty of a blossom. The grace of a high-flying bird. The roar of wind in the trees: At one time or another in our lives, nature touches...all of us in some personal, special way. Her immense mystery opens to us a little of its stunning purity, reminding us of a Life that is greater than the little affairs of man."[2]

Taking a close look at nature is becoming more and more difficult in modern urban areas. Buildings and pavement have replaced woods and fields, fish cannot be seen in murky, polluted rivers and streams, while smog and city lights obscure the splendor of the night sky. Even in Montessori's time, real encounters with nature were becoming infrequent. She laments, "In the civilized environment of our society, children live far from nature, and have few opportunities of entering into intimate contact with it." Does anyone, she asks, "let them run out when it is raining, take off their shoes when they find pools of water, and let them run about with bare feet when the grass of the meadow is damp with dew?"[3]

Today this deprivation has dramatically increased. Unstructured outdoor play where children climb trees and make mud pies has all but disappeared. One can walk the streets on weekend afternoons or early summer evenings and never hear the joyous shouts of youngsters playing freely in the outdoors. Instead one finds the children at organized sports, indoor skating, ballet classes or most often in front of the television.

Contact with nature is further hindered because some youngsters are over-stimulated with too many toys, too many scheduled activities and too many high-tech products. Interest in nature pales for the child who has her own phone, TV, stereo and/or computer in her bedroom. Where are the quiet moments just to look out the window, to be awed by a humming bird, to imagine, to question and to dream?

[2] Joseph Cornell, *Sharing Nature With Children*, p. 8.

[3] Maria Montessori, *The Discovery of the Child*, p. 100.

As contact with nature decreases, the child's capacity for wonder becomes seriously undernourished and his fledgling spirit can begin to wither. Montessori grieves,"How often is the soul of man, — especially that of the child — deprived because one does not put him into contact with nature."[4]

Perhaps no other book so beautifully inspires adults to keep alive this delicate capacity in children as *The Sense of Wonder* by the late Rachel Carson. She describes sharing nature with her very young grandnephew, Roger, making no conscious effort to teach him names of plants, birds or insects but simply expressing her own pleasure in what they encountered on their long walks.

Year after year Ms. Carson took Roger on walks in the Maine woods — often in the rain — and let him share her enjoyment of "things people ordinarily deny children because they are inconvenient, interfering with bedtime, or involving wet clothing that has to be changed or mud that has to be cleaned off the rug." Setting aside these concerns in favor of meaningful experiences for Roger, she writes, "We have let him join us in the dark living room...to watch the full moon riding lower and lower toward the far shore of the bay, setting all the water ablaze with silver flames...because the memory of that scene would mean more to him in manhood than the sleep he was losing...

"If I had influence with the good fairy," she continues, "who is supposed to preside over the christening of all children I should ask that her gift to each child in the world be a sense of wonder so indestructible that it would last throughout life, as an unfailing antidote against the boredom and disenchantments of later years, the sterile preoccupation with things that are artificial, the alienation from the sources of our strength.

"If a child is to keep alive his inborn sense of wonder without any such gift from the fairies, he needs the companionship of at least one adult who can share it, rediscovering with him the joy, excitement and mystery of the world we live in."

Anticipating the uneasiness this task may bring to some adults who don't "know one bird from another," Ms. Carson assures us that, "It is not

---

[4] Maria Montessori, *From Childhood to Adolescence*, p. 35.

half so important to *know* as to *feel*...If facts are the seeds that later produce knowledge and wisdom, then the emotions and the impressions of the senses are the fertile soil in which the seeds must grow. The years of early childhood are the time to prepare the soil."[5]

NURTURING WONDER IN THE SCHOOL YARD

Ms. Carson's advice is particularly relevant to Montessori teachers of young children. With as many outdoor delights as possible these teachers can help to keep alive the child's clear-eyed vision — that true instinct for what is beautiful and awe-inspiring and can awaken children's natural curiosity that leads to seeking factual knowledge. Youngsters who have climbed up to see a bird's nest, watched worms moving without any legs, delighted in tadpoles or turned over an old log in the woods to find life swarming beneath it, will, for example, be more eager to classify vertebrate and invertebrate animals when studying cosmic education than children who have never had such experiences. Rudolf Steiner insisted, "It is absolutely essential that before we begin to think, before we so much as begin to set our thinking in motion, we experience the condition of wonder."[6]

Sofia Cavalletti, too, credits the power of wonder for enticing children into deeper study. "Wonder is not a force that pushes us passively from behind; it is situated ahead of us with irresistible force toward the object of our astonishment; it makes us advance toward it, filled with enchantment."[7]

But how can we give children this experience with nature, particularly in our urban schools? In an ideal world, every school would be located on several acres of ground with a stand of beautiful trees, a field to explore, a pond to observe, a sunny garden and even room to care for a few farm animals such as chickens or sheep. Such schools do exist. Recently I visited a semi-rural Waldorf school where each class had a vegetable garden complete with a scarecrow the children had made. The

---

[5] Rachael Carson, *The Sense of Wonder*, pp. 22, 42, 43, 45.

[6] Rudolph Steiner, quoted by Joan Alman in, "Education For Creative Thinking: The Waldorf Approach," *Revision*, Vol. 15, No. 2, p.74.

[7] Sofia Cavalletti, *The Religious Potential of the Child*, p. 38.

eight year-olds, with their fathers, had built a chicken coop with a little door in the back through which the children retrieved eggs every morning. Their compost pile was covered with a sign in a child's handwriting, "Do not disturb. A miracle is taking place." These children were obviously in awe of nature's way of turning food scraps and leaves into plant-nourishing fertilizer.

Most teachers, however, are not fortunate enough to have the luxury of undeveloped land surrounding them. Nevertheless, if nurturing wonder is a priority, a teacher in any school can call children's attention to the marvels of nature in whatever outdoor space is available, no matter how small.

For example, you don't need several acres for cloud watching. All you need is a warm day when clouds are moving and a clear space where children can lie on the ground and watch. They will delight as they recognize bears, pillows, turtles, ships and giants in the sky.

Let the children revel in this experience. Later talk to them about how clouds give us rain that flows into streams, rivers, gulfs and oceans. Remarkably some of the water evaporates and rises again to form clouds. What a wondrous journey gives us the water we need for life on earth! How awesome that nature recycles water for us! What are all the things we need water for? Could we live without water?

Interesting discoveries are often made, not when we have new landscapes to look at, but when we have new eyes to look at what we see every day. Fostering children's sense of wonder means helping them to slow down and to linger in their observations of all that surrounds them.

For Spacious Skies,[8] an organization dedicated to increasing awareness of the sky, suggests this activity for young school children. Draw the blinds in the classroom or take them into a room with no windows such as an inside hallway or auditorium. Ask, "How many of you saw the sky this morning?" Probably all will raise their hands. Then give the children paper and crayons and ask them to draw what the sky looks like today. Is it white, light grey, dark grey, black, pale blue, bright blue? Are there no clouds, a few clouds, many clouds? Is the sun shining? Can you see the moon?

[8] *For Spacious Skies,* 54 Webb Street, Lexington, MA 02173

Next take the group outside and let them actually observe today's sky. Then return to the classroom and ask the children to make a new drawing of the sky they just saw. The differences in their before and after drawings will help them to learn how to observe something carefully that they see every day but don't always look at with complete attention.

Betsy Hoke, director of The Montessori Children's House of Evergreen, CO, is a great advocate of "getting children outside away from computers and TV." The average schoolyard, she feels, offers many opportunities because young children are often more interested in small details than in tremendous landscapes. She recalls driving a group of children to see a great panoramic view of the mountains and the first comment she heard was, "Look at that bug squished on the windshield."

Betsy suggests periodic walks around the school yard to pick up small objects that can be sorted into *living* and *non-living* categories — leaves, weeds, flowers, blades of grass, worms, ants, stones, pieces of trash such as bottle caps and bits of paper. This activity is good for picking up litter as well as an introduction to classification.

For areas that have seasonal changes, Betsy says, it is interesting to rope off for observation a small area of the school yard that has some growing things. A class of children can formally visit this area once a month and note the seasonal variations in a journal. Photographs can be taken periodically and placed on a Time Line. This will show how the same area looks in late summer, early fall, late fall, winter, early spring and late spring — a school-year observation of a cycle of nature!

"If there is only one interesting path that is convenient for outdoor walks," Mark Ross, a teacher at Mt. Scopis Montessori School in Carbondale, CO, says, "you can take the children on the same path several times — each time with a different focus. On one trip they can look for different types of stones; the next trip for various flowers; the next trip for different kinds of trees; and in the fall for different kinds of leaves on the ground."

It is worthwhile for the nature-oriented teacher and her class to plant berry bushes in the school yard that will attract birds. A good choice is a bayberry bush that produces berries in early spring. For the winter months hang wire containers filled with suet and bird feeders filled with seed in places where they can be seen from classroom windows. I particularly recommend a bird feeder mounted on a one-way glass that can be attached with suction cups to the outside of a window. This enables the children to observe the feeding bird at close range because the special glass prevents the bird from seeing the children who are just inches away.

In the spring, drop a few nest-building items in the schoolyard, such as small strips of old soft rags or pieces of straw to encourage birds to build nests nearby. Listening to bird calls is a good sensorial exercise, especially in spring. Have the children sit or lie down in the school yard. Tell them to close their eyes, to be very quiet and to hold their arms out with fists closed. Each time they hear a *new* bird call they raise one finger.

Hang pictures in the classroom of birds that are common in your area and let the children keep a record of which birds they see in the school yard. It is interesting to note the first and last sightings of migrating birds, such as robins, that move to warmer climates in the winter and return in the spring. How remarkable that they know when to migrate! How phenomenal that they know which direction to fly and when and how to return! Many fly to the same location every year. Children can wonder, as have scientists, about this extraordinary ability.

A common activity for fall in the small school yard is planting bulbs (daffodils, tulips, crocuses) that will bloom in the spring and planting seeds in the spring (marigolds, asters, mums, zinnias) that will be blooming when the children return to school in September. When children plant they come into intimate contact with the soil — a firsthand experience of Mother Earth.

Many teachers have planting activities for the children, but the spiritually aware teacher adds another dimension. He or she calls the children's attention to the miracle of growth, asking them questions such as: What made the beautiful color of this flower? Could you make a bulb that would grow into a flower? Can you make yourself grow five inches in two weeks? How did the little seed do that? Be careful not to over-whelm a spiritual moment with too many questions. Reserve some of them for later when the group is reflecting on the experience.

Trees are one of nature's greatest gifts to us, but one that children often take for granted. "There is no description, no image in any book," Montessori writes, "that is capable of replacing the sight of real trees, and all the life to be found around them, in a real forest. Something emanates from those trees that speaks to the soul, something no book, no museum is capable of giving...and which no one can bring into the school."[9]

In his nature awareness guidebook, Joseph Cornell suggests that teachers teach less and share more. "Besides telling children the bare facts of nature, 'This is a mountain hemlock tree,' I like to tell them about my inner feelings in the presence of that hemlock tree. I tell them about my awe and respect for the way a hemlock can survive in sub-alpine conditions—where water is scarce in summer, and mostly frozen in winter; where harsh winter winds twist and bend and kill its branches...

"Children respond to my observations much more freely than they respond to textbook explanations. Take the case of a hemlock tree that...sits between two huge boulders near a camp...It had to send its roots down 25 feet to reach the rocky soil below. The children would frequently make a detour on their hikes just to empty their canteens by its roots... In fact, [each year] as soon as they arrived at camp they would run out to see how it fared through the dry autumn and cold winter."[10]

A setting in the woods is an ideal place to have children ponder the vitally important role of trees on our planet. If it is not possible to take the children to a woodsy area, the trees in the school yard, or even one special tree in the neighborhood, can be the focus of this experience. After a short period of silent reflection ask the children to name the gifts that trees give to us. The list can be impressive: beauty; cool shade on hot days; pine cones; many kinds of fruit; various nuts; rubber; cork; resins; maple syrup; wood for building and for burning to keep warm; pulp for everything that's made of paper, including newspapers and books; leaves that make oxygen for us and then fall to the ground to make fertilizer; roots that keep our fertile soil from washing away (areas without trees often become deserts). Trees protect us from dust storms. They offer a leafy home to owls, birds, squirrels, insects and children who like to climb on their branches.

We can look at an old tree and know that it was standing when our great-grandparents were little children. We can look at the inside of a tree

---

[9] Maria Montessori, *From Childhood to Adolescence*, p.35.

[10] Joseph Cornell, *Sharing Nature With Children*, p. 11-13.

trunk that has been cross cut and count the rings to find out how old it was — one ring for each year. We can roll over a rotting tree trunk or log and see that, even after it has died, this tree is still providing a home and nourishment for many insects that live in the forest. Trees have many tasks on our planet; they perform them well.

When nourishing the sense of wonder, it is important to help children to become aware that all nature moves in cycles. So mindful of this were the Native Americans that the symbol of the circle was sacred to them. They chose to build their tepees in a shape that was round at the bottom where it touched the earth and their tepees were arranged in a huge circle that they called the *hoop of the nation*. "Everything an Indian does is in a circle ...because the Power of the World always works in circles and everything tries to be round...The earth is round like a ball...The wind, in its greatest power, whirls. Birds make their nests in circles...The sun comes forth and goes down again in a circle ...The moon does the same and both are round. Even the seasons form a great circle in their changing, and always come back again to where they were. The life of a man is a circle from childhood to childhood, and so it is in everything where power moves."[11]

Children can become aware of the monthly cycle of the moon; the cycle of the day and night as the earth rotates on its axis; the cycle of plant life from putting a seed in the ground, to sprouting, to growth, to flowering, to the death of the flower, to the producing of new seed. A child who understands the marvelous way that nature operates in cycles will eventually see his or her own life as part of this system of cycles and may then feel more comfortable with death, realizing that all life comes to an end so new life can begin.

---

[11] John G. Neihardt, *Black Elk Speaks*, pp. 194-195.

Chapter 11

EXPERIENCING WONDER IN THE CLASSROOM

The child's sense of wonder can also be nourished inside the classroom with activities that have been thoughtfully prepared to arouse curiosity.

The many rainbows that appear in children's drawings tell us how fascinated children are with this beautiful array of colors that in many religious faiths symbolizes hope, promise and blessing. How perceptive of young children to choose this symbol for their spontaneous art work! Something as simple as a crystal hanging in a sunny window can build on this fascination and lead to interesting speculation about the rainbows it forms in the air. Children will try to catch them with their hands and they will be disappointed on cloudy days when the rainbows do not appear. Joan Gilbert reports, "After many overcast days in February, the sun emerged. For the younger children it was as if the rainbows appeared for the first time, even though the crystal had been hanging up since fall. They enthusiastically brought me over to see."

THE WONDER OF LIGHT

It is fun to talk about the wonder of the rainbow. Where do the colors come from? Are they really hidden inside light? Are there other things in life that are hidden but we know they are there? Where does light come from? Is it a gift to us? What would happen if we had no light? Could we see anything? Could plants grow? Would we have any food?

Joan has designed a shelf exercise to deepen the child's wonder at how light passing through a prism reveals the mysteriously hidden colors of the spectrum and to learn the order of these colors. The materials for the first part of this exercise consist of a prism mounted on a stand (available in catalogs of science materials) and six small clear glass bottles (such as eye-dropper bottles) filled with water tinted with food coloring — one for each of the primary colors, red, blue and yellow and one for each of the secondary colors — orange, purple and green. All bottle caps are sealed tightly.

These materials are on a white tray that the child carries to a sunlit spot in the classroom. First the child carefully observes the rainbow that appears on the white tray when the sun shines through the prism. Then she lines up the glass bottles in the same order as the colors in the spectrum. When the sun shines through the bottles it forms a second rainbow on the white tray.

The materials for the next part of the exercise consist of a set of colored pencils and white paper on which the children can duplicate the rainbow formed by the prism.

INFINITY

"One day," Joan tells us, "a five year-old child took a large piece of easel paper, folded it in half, and began writing numbers at a table, commenting that he was making a book of all the numbers. He was later joined by two others with their papers and this work continued for two days. On the 3rd day, the first child excitedly showed me his papers full of numbers and announced that he was writing his 'infinities.'

"When we gathered in circle, I invited him to tell about his work. I mentioned that "infinity" is a word that means to continue without ending, and that many people think there is no end to numbers. I invited the children in turn to say the highest number they could think of; then I would say the next number. Soon older ones caught on and began offering the next number.

"I commented that it is hard to imagine infinity, and was immediately contradicted by enthusiastic voices saying, 'No, it isn't hard!' This surprising response led me to believe that because of children's great capacity for wonder and simple embracing of mysteries, it is probably easier for them than for me to imagine infinity."

SNOWFLAKES

An art activity commonly presented as an extension of cutting exercises is the making of "snowflakes" out of folded paper. "Before presenting this activity," Joan says, "I sit with the children and ponder the marvel of snowflakes.

"I wonder how many snowflakes have ever fallen from the sky? Do you think anyone could ever count them all? Do you think even everyone together could count them? They all seem to be alike ...but do you know that when scientists put them under microscopes, they found that each was amazingly and beautifully different?" (Show photos if possible.) "Are any of us exactly the same? Will any two of our snowflakes that we cut out be exactly the same?"

The materials for this activity are: White bond paper, 6" square, good quality child's scissors, glue, 7" circle of dark blue paper and a tray.

The child takes the tray with the materials to a table and folds one piece of the 6" square paper three times, carefully matching the corners. He then cuts the folded paper in a random pattern. He unfolds it and admires the design that resembles an enlarged snowflake. He glues it onto the blue background sheet and disposes of the scraps.

As a variation of this activity the child can use his "snowflake" as a stencil for printing with a sponge and blue tempera on white paper or with fabric paint on cloth.

Each child's "snowflake" will be different from those made by other children. When the class looks at an array of these it reminds them of one of the marvels of nature — no two snowflakes look alike.

PLANTS

Planting activities in the classroom can serve two purposes related to the child's spirit. The actual sprouting of a seed can fill children with wonder, and caring for that seed and the plant that results can teach children a sense of responsibility toward the world of nature.

To enhance the children's perception of the miraculous power that seeds have to sprout, try this little experiment when children are planting seeds in small containers filled with earth. In three or four of the containers let the children plant something other than seeds such as a penny or a button. Label these carefully. Water them regularly and put them in a sunny spot with the other containers that are labeled as particular kinds of seeds. Let the children analyze the results.

In another experiment have the children plant seeds in two containers of dry soil. Place one of them in a sunny spot but do not water it at all. Put the second one in a dark place, such as a closet or drawer, and water it regularly. The results will show the necessity for light and moisture that nature provides for successful growth of plants. What happens when we deprive the seeds of either one of these gifts of nature?

Children who are intrigued by the mystery of a living plant emerging from a tiny seed can be motivated to care for plants, to make charts of plant growth, to learn the parts of a plant, the needs of a plant and the many ways that plants meet the needs of people.

"Solicitous care for living things affords satisfaction to one of the most lively instincts of the child's mind," Montessori tells us.[1] When a child knows that a little plant will dry up if he does not water it or that an animal needs him to bring it food and water, the child begins to develop a sense of responsibility for other living things. With careful nurturing this youthful concern can grow into a deep respect for the interdependence of people and nature.

For example, when working with plants, tell the children that plants give us the oxygen that we breathe and we give plants the carbon dioxide that they need. While plants quietly grow in the sunlight, the chlorophyll in their green leaves absorbs the carbon dioxide that we exhale and turns it into oxygen for us to breathe again. This is called *photosynthesis*. Without it all people would die from lack of oxygen. Talking about this wondrous exchange that is basic to all life instills in children an awe of the balance of nature.

DOVES

Joan Gilbert reminds us that Maria Montessori mentions the value of allowing children to care for plants and animals that have symbolic roles, such as the dove which often represents peace.

---

[1] Maria Montessori, *Discovery of the Child*, p. 103.

"In the fall, I set up a large cage in a corner of the classroom which became home for a pair of ringneck doves. In January, the female laid two eggs, which were cared for by both parents. Two weeks later the eggs hatched, and we were able to enjoy watching the growth and nurturing of two baby doves by both parents.

"A record of the days from the time the first egg was laid until they hatched was kept by one child who spent more hours than the rest of us put together observing the doves.

"I took photos at one week intervals from when the eggs were laid until the young doves were independent and could fly at one month old. From this I made a timeline.

"I can't begin to assess or express all we've received from the presence of the doves in our classroom. They do embody the peacefulness they symbolically represent. They are gentle and harmless, and not easily upset. They are subtly affectionate towards each other. The sounds they make have a pleasant beauty. Together they built the nest, cared for the eggs, kept the newly hatched babies warm, and fed them.

"We all had an opportunity to hope together that the eggs would hatch, to be amazed at the wonder of new life when they did, and to witness the miracle of growth and change as the featherless protected hatchlings became birds who could fly, almost the size of their parents."

Close observation of birds can spawn many questions for the children to ponder — "What can birds do that you can't do?" "Could you leave your home when you were one month old?" "How do the birds know that they have to sit on the eggs to keep them warm?"

THE DEATH OF A PET

Just as children can experience the excitement of new life in the classroom, they also are sometimes saddened by the death of a classroom pet. Since death is a natural part of the cycle of life, it should not be hidden from the children. Children, like adults, naturally wonder about death. It is helpful for them to have an opportunity to voice their questions, to speculate on what happens after death and to freely express their grief.

Judy Paulsen, now a pre-primary teacher at Giving Tree Montessori School in Colorado Springs, CO, writes, "A few years ago our guinea pig,

Cookie, died at school. Since she had been a cherished pet for all of us for five years, we gathered together to celebrate her life and mourn her death. First we laid her body on her rug so all the children could see her and we encouraged them to express how they were feeling. Almost every child and teacher told how sad he or she was.

"I next read them *Badger's Parting Gifts*,[2] the best children's book I know of on this subject. We all talked of different and special moments that we had had with Cookie.

"The children spent several hours decorating a shoe box and we put Cookie's body into this box that they had lovingly prepared. Beside it we placed small baskets of flowers, seashells, and pretty stones. Each child then put either a stone, shell or flower in the box with Cookie. We buried her in the school yard.

"During the next few days I read the children *The 10th Good Thing About Barney*[3] and *The Fall of Freddie the Leaf*.[4] Together we planted a small aspen tree on the grave where we had buried Cookie. I explained that her body would help the tree grow and we would remember Cookie whenever we looked at this tree near our school. The children accepted this peacefully. Then we sang,

> 'It's alright to cry,
> Crying gets the sad out of you,
> Raindrops from your eyes,
> Might make you feel better.[5]

BUTTERFLIES

Another very interesting cycle of life that children can observe is the *metamorphosis* of the caterpillar into the butterfly.

Mary Truesdale, a Montessori teacher at Penn-Mont Academy, Altoona, PA, suggests letting this process happen in the classroom. A see-through box with a coupon to send for caterpillars is available in nature

---

[2] Susan Varley, *Badger's Parting Gifts*.

[3] Judith Viorst, *The 10th Good Thing About Barney*.

[4] Leo Buscaglia, *The Fall of Freddie the Leaf*.

[5] *It's Alright to Cry* from Marlo Thomas and Friends album, *Free to be . . . You and Me*.

stores and through catalogs. Her students fed the caterpillars and marvelled at how quickly they grew fat. Then they observed the caterpillars climbing to the top of the see-through box, wiggling a great deal and spinning their chrysalis. They were absolutely awed when the beautiful butterflies emerged a few weeks later. It was an ideal time for questions touching on the mystery of death. "What happened to the caterpillar that was inside the *chrysalis*?" "Did it die?" "Where did the butterfly come from?" "Was it a part of the caterpillar that we couldn't see?"

If wonder becomes a fundamental attitude in a child's life it will confer on him or her a spiritual character, because wonder constantly reminds all of us of the mysteries of reality. There is hardly anything beautiful or powerful in nature that is not touched by some mysterious, unfathomable or transcendent characteristic. Whenever possible the spiritually aware teacher directs the children's attention to an object of wonder and marvels with them at the miracles it represents. Why not make more room for this spiritual dimension in our classrooms? Why not give it precedence in the activities we select and make it a recurring theme in discussions with children?

"Wonder is an exceedingly important stimulus for the human spirit," Sofia Cavalletti writes. "[It] can arise only from an attentive observation of reality. Education to wonder is correlative with an education that helps us to go always more deeply into reality. If we skim over things we will never be surprised by them. Wonder is not an emotion of superficial people; it strikes root only in the person whose mind is able to settle and rest in things; in the person who is capable of stopping and looking."[6]

---

[6] Sofia Cavalletti, *The Religious Potential of the Child*, pp. 138-139.

Chapter 12

THE SPIRITUAL MEANING OF
COSMIC EDUCATION

*Let us give the child a vision of the
whole universe...for all things are part of the universe,
and are connected with each other to form one whole unity.*

Maria Montessori[1]

*Our primary teacher is the universe.
The universe evokes our being, supplies us with creative energy,
insists on a reverent attitude toward everything,
and liberates us from our puny self-definition.*

Brian Swimme[2]

Maria Montessori was ahead of her time when she placed cosmic education as the centerpiece of her elementary program. While other educators were teaching history as a series of wars and a succession of monarchies, she began with the miracle of the cosmos, filling the children with a great sense of awe as one by one they encountered all the wonders of creation that preceded them in history.

Essentially Montessori's cosmic education gives the child first an all-encompassing sense of the universe with its billions of galaxies. Then it focuses on our galaxy, the Milky Way, our solar system, planet Earth and its geological history, the first specimens of life, all species of plants

---

[1] Maria Montessori, *To Educate the Human Potential,* p. 8.

[2] Brian Swimme, *The Universe is a Green Dragon,* p. 167.

and animals and finally human beings. Inherent in the whole study is the interconnectedness of all creation, the oneness of all things, the relative newness of the human race.

In this chapter, instead of offering several new activities for cosmic education, I want to explore its spiritual roots and its spiritual consequences. Montessori's concept of cosmic education is, perhaps, her most valuable educational legacy. However, it is not always presented in its totality. Some practitioners have extracted the charts, drawings, clocks, time lines, etc. from their philosophical base and have ignored the awesome implications of an unfolding universe. In my opinion, this has deprived the curriculum of its mystical essence — a cosmic view of life.

The word *cosmic* comes from the Greek word *cosmos*. Contrary to a common assumption, the word *cosmos* is not an exact synonym for the word *universe*. Webster's primary definition of *universe* is "all created things viewed as constituting one system or whole." His definition of *cosmos* is "the universe conceived as an orderly and harmonious system; contrasted with chaos."[3] The distinction is important because the "order" that is inherent in the word *cosmos* implies a plan in which all nature and all people are a part of its unfolding.

Montessori chose the word *cosmic* rather than *universal* for her preeminent elementary curriculum because she did believe that the universe was an orderly and harmonious system. "[Everything is] correlated to a central idea, of greatly enabling inspiration — the Cosmic Plan, in which all, consciously or unconsciously, serve the great Purpose of Life."[4]

Montessori first began her work on cosmic education in the early 1930's. However, she developed the major portion of it, particularly the underlying principles, while in India with her son, Mario, from 1939 to 1946. As Italians, interned in India by the British government for the duration of World War II, the Montessoris were unable to continue their usual schedule of international travel. Although Maria Montessori gave many lectures and training courses (with Mario translating from Italian to English) she lived a quieter and more reflective existence amidst the Indian culture.

---

[3] Webster, op. cit.

[4] Maria Montessori, *To Educate the Human Potential*, p. 2.

According to Sister Christina Trudeau, "During her seven year stay in India, Montessori's concepts about human life and culture [underwent] some important alterations. The scope of her view absorbed the thinking of two world traditions...both the Western scientific outlook and the spiritual insights of Eastern thought."[5]

Montessori's cosmic education rests on the concept of evolution — a theory that contains many scientific facts and is widely accepted but not absolutely proven. In modern usage biological evolution refers to the theory that the various types of animals and plants have their origin in other pre-existing types; that they are the descendants of a very few simple organisms (or perhaps of but one); and that due to gradual modifications in successive generations, the higher forms of life are derived from the lower. Geological evolution goes back much further, holding that everything in the universe beginning with the stars came forth from the same atoms in the great original fireball.

Among elementary students in a Montessori school there may be children whose families reject evolution in favor of the biblical story of creation or the theory that everything in the universe came about simply by chance. Therefore in non-sectarian classrooms it is wise to show respect for the positions of others by explaining that evolution is a possible explanation of the origin of the world but that some people hold other beliefs.

To illustrate this, Mary Lou Kane, a Montessori teacher at Penn-Mont Academy, reads several creation stories — Native American, African, Chinese, Inuit, Old Testament — to her elementary class while they are studying evolution. If they ask which one is true, she responds that there may be some truth in each of them. She encourages her students to ponder the stories as others have done for thousands of years.

Mary Lou also points out to them that our understanding of the universe has changed many times with new discoveries. The great astronomer, Ptolemy, in the second century placed a motionless earth at the center of the universe with the moon, sun and planets going around it. He believed that the stars were brilliant spots of light in a concave dome that arched over everything. Fourteen hundred years later

[5] Sister Christina Marie Trudeau, *Montessori's Years in India*, pp. 67-68.

Copernicus founded present day astronomy with his theory that the earth and the planets revolve around the sun. In the third century B.C.E. Aristotle postulated that the moon was a smooth sphere shining by its own light. Galileo, in the 17th century observed that its surface was marked by valleys and mountains and that it showed only the light it reflected from the sun. His observations indicated that the Milky Way was a mass of stars "so numerous as to be almost beyond belief."

David Kahn, Executive Director of the North American Teacher's Association, calls attention to three levels of the evolutionary concept: fact, theory and philosophy. There is little question that evolution is based on facts, but the interpretation of these facts entails various levels of reality and conjecture that have generated years of intense debate. The intent of Montessori's cosmic education, Kahn believes, is purely philosophical. "Quite clearly the facts of evolution are secondary. Montessori looks at this broad scope of evolving life on earth as a philosophy which evokes the imagination of the child to look through space and time, to build a fiery enthusiasm for the organization of life, to build a moral vision where judgment is enhanced by nature's book of connected ideas."[6]

Kahn's conclusions echo Montessori's own words: "To interest the children in the universe, we must *not* begin by giving them elementary facts about it, to make them merely understand its mechanism, but start with far loftier notions of a philosophical nature, put in an acceptable manner, suited to the child's psychology."[7]

Montessori's view of evolution is similar to the views held by many modern scientists and was supported by discoveries made after her death. Revolutionary advances such as those in physics, aerodynamics, astronomy, photography and communications have revealed that the universe is not a static phenomena, as was previously believed, but is still evolving and is dynamically alive: a whole system, fluid and interrelated.

"Most amazing is this realization," physicist Brian Swimme writes, "that everything that exists in the universe came from a common origin. The material of your body and the material of my body are intrinsically related because they emerged from and are caught up in a single ener-

---

[6] David Kahn, "Cosmic Education: Sowing Life, Not theories" *NAMTA Journal*, Spring 1988, pp. 80-87

[7] Maria Montessori, *To Educate the Human Potential*, p. 29.

getic event. Our ancestry stretches back through the life forms and into the stars, back to the beginnings of the primeval fireball. This universe is a single multiform energetic unfolding of matter, mind, intelligence, and life."[8]

John Fowler, an upper elementary teacher at Mitchell Montessori School in Denver, has created a *Time Line of Light* inspired by the new cosmologies. With dramatic illustrations this Time Line depicts the evolution of the universe and life on earth in a stunningly fluent and beautiful manner, consistent with current theory and discovery. "As a major premise from which the sciences unfurl, the material offers a holistic vision," John says, "from the perspective of the origin and evolution of the galaxies, bacteria, niches,[9] and biological relationships as they first appeared."

John's work follows Montessori's advice to "regard the child's intelligence as a fertile field in which seeds may be sown, to grow under the heat of flaming imagination."[10] Before showing his students this unusual Time Line, John asks them to close their eyes while he reads them an imaginative story of the beginnings of the universe. Then the children respond by drawing or painting what they imagined during the reading.[11]

What spiritual insights can be gained from the study of cosmic education? I believe that the following concepts emanate from a modern view of the cosmos. They can give all of us a more hopeful and meaningful perspective on life.

PEACE

If everything in the universe came about from the same source — the original fireball that many believe preceded the creation of the stars — then we as human beings are related to all other human beings, as well as to the animals, plants, oceans and heavenly bodies. Therefore if we deliberately destroy nature or harm other living beings we might be ultimately destroying ourselves. This realization is an underlying principle for promoting peace, equality and care of the earth.

---

[8] Brian Swimme, *The Universe is a Green Dragon*, p. 28.

[9] Niche — the position or function of an organism in a community of plants and animals.

[10] Maria Montessori, *To Educate the Human Potential*, p. 15.

[11] For further information on *A Time Line of Light* contact John Fowler, 28887 Clover Lane, Evergreen, CO 80439.

CONSERVATION

We can never throw anything "away" because there is no such place as "away." There is only the universe — home to us all. This realization could be the underlying principle for conservation, the wise use and reuse of man-made things and the potential harm of excessive productivity and accumulation.

VALUES

Of all the levels of evolution, human beings are the only known species on earth that can reflect on creation. As the most highly developed form of life on Earth, we make it possible for the universe to know and feel itself through our awareness. From this point of view, the people who are most valuable to the universe are not the most wealthy or the most athletic, but those who are awake to its splendor and who ignite this kind of awareness in others.

HOPE

Cosmic education can give us all a sense of hope. "Hope," Sofia Cavalletti tells us, "is that dynamism that urges us to view the reality in which we are immersed in a positive manner."[12] Despite all the violence in the universe — fireball, enormous explosions, meteors colliding with planets — and all the violence on Planet Earth — hurricanes, volcanic eruptions, earthquakes, tornadoes, wars — life has continued to progress in a relentless fashion. When we observe this long view of cosmic history, we do not see regression in the universe; we see life constantly moving toward an ever higher degree of complexity.

GRATITUDE

When we deepen our awareness of the universe, we feel fresh gratitude for the billions of years of evolutionary labor that gave us human life and for the thousands of years of human labor that gave us modern technology. As examples, when we see a beautiful valley nestled in the mountains, we can reflect on the fact that it was formed by water that labored thousands of years to wear down the earth; when we enter a car or a train, we can look back and feel grateful to the first human being who

---

[12] Sofia Cavalletti, *Catechesis of the Good Shepherd 1989-90 Newsletter*, p.5.

constructed a wheel. Awareness of the long-term cosmic pattern, of which we are only an infinitesimal part, calls us to a deep humility and reverence for all the labors of nature and the work of human beings that preceded us.

OPENNESS

The realization that the cosmos is not static, that it is still unfolding, bids us to be open to new possibilities. What is the next step in the ongoing evolution? Is it a spiritual one, rather than a physical one? Are we converging toward a spiritual unity — an omega point — as Teilhard de Chardin suggested? As cosmic educators we do not have to believe that such spiritual phenomena will come about but we should not rule out any spiritual phenomena, such as extrasensory perception, that may be a harbinger of the future of evolution.

COSMIC TASK

Perhaps the most significant spiritual benefit of cosmic education is that it gives both children and adults a sense of purpose in their lives — a sense of belonging to an entity much greater than themselves, in which they can play an important part. Montessori called this role a cosmic task, meaning a significant individual contribution to the unfolding of the universe.

In *To Educate The Human Potential*, the book about cosmic education that she wrote while in India, Montessori claimed that all forms of life have a dual purpose. The first is for self-preservation, growth and survival of the species. "Another—and stronger—factor in evolutionary processes is concerned with the cosmic function of each living being, and even of inanimate natural objects, working in collaboration for the fulfill-ment of the Purpose of Life."

Trees and plants, she explains, naturally seek sunshine and carbon dioxide for their nourishment, unconscious that the cosmos has given them these instinctual urges for the purpose of preserving the purity of the air. The bee who takes nectar from a flower is driven only by his own need; he is unconscious of the role he is playing to perpetuate that species of flower.

"Man too, like all beings, has the two purposes, conscious and unconscious. He is conscious of his own intellectual and physical needs, and of the claims on him of society and civilization. He...has yet to become conscious of his far deeper responsibilities to a cosmic task, his collaboration with others in work[ing] for his environment, for the whole universe."[13]

A human being is led to his or her cosmic task by an allurement, that is, by an authentic passion or interest that emanates from the true self. Brian Swimme writes, "We awake to our own unique set of attractions. So do oxygen atoms. So do protons. The proton is attracted only to certain particles. On an infinitely more complex level, the same holds true for humans: Each person discovers a field of allurements, the totality of which bears the unique stamp of the person's personality. Destiny unfolds in the pursuit of individual fascinations and interests."[14]

In Swimme's viewpoint, various allurements — gravitational, chemical, electromagnetic, biological, sexual etc. — form the fundamental dynamic of the unfolding cosmos. Without gravitational allurement, the galaxies, the solar system and the earth itself would break apart and we would float off into space. Reflecting on this gives us some idea of the tremendous importance of allurements. They are not only the cohesive force in the universe, they are the magnetism or pulling power that keep it constantly evolving. Allurements, he believes, are responsible for the evolution and continuation of every species.

Joseph Campbell speaks of the importance of personal allurements. "Each incarnation, you might say, has a potentiality and the mission of life is to live that potentiality. How do you do it? My answer is 'Follow your bliss.'"[15]

How do we as teachers help children to follow their bliss, or in other words, to find their authentic interests? Montessori took two important steps in this direction. She recognized and described sensitive periods in children. These are periods of intense fascination (allurement) for learning a particular skill, such as to speak a language or to climb steps. It is easier for a child to learn a particular skill during the corresponding sensitive period than at any other time in his or her life. By making

---

[13] Maria Montessori, *To Educate the Human Potential*, p. 42.

[14] Brian Swimme, *The Universe is a Green Dragon*, p. 47.

[15] Joseph Campbell with Bill Moyers, *The Power of Myth*, p. 229

parents and teachers aware of these sensitive periods, Montessori enhanced children's opportunities to follow their natural allurements. She again gave children this opportunity in the classroom where they were allowed and encouraged to choose their own work, thus taking advantage of their instinctive periods of interest. She firmly believed that "a child chooses what helps him to construct himself."[16]

A child's passion of interest, that may eventually lead to meaningful work, is a precious personal desire that is sometimes squelched by the powerful influence of parents, teachers, peer groups, cultural trends, the media or perceived obligations. When Montessori talked about nourishing the child's spirit, she was referring, I believe, to preserving this delicate inner core that holds the secret of the cosmic task that will make each child's life meaningful and satisfying.

If children can see their own lives in the framework of the cosmos, if each one can see the role he or she must play in its unfolding, life will become more meaningful. As we encourage children to act from their authentic center rather than to be swayed by peer groups, or passing fads, we will free them to follow their bliss — to work on and enjoy what is most meaningful to them.

The value of cosmic education, as I see it, is that it places the child's life in a spiritual perspective. No one can be confronted with the cosmic miracle and not see that there is more to life than our everyday experience. Fast foods, designer sneakers, video games and sports heroes all pale beside the wonder of the universe.

"If the idea of the universe would be presented to the child in the right way," Montessori wrote, "it will create in him admiration and wonder...The stars, earth, stones, life of all kinds form a whole in relation with each other, and so close is this relation that we cannot understand a stone without some understanding of the great sun! The child begins to ask, 'How did it come into being, and how will it end?' 'What am I?' 'What is our task in this wonderful universe?' 'Do we merely live here for ourselves, or is there something more for us to do?'"[17] Ultimately these are spiritual questions and pursuing them is a spiritual quest, perhaps the most important challenge of cosmic education.

[16] Maria Montessori, *The Absorbent Mind*, p. 223.

[17] Maria Montessori, *To Educate the Human Potential*, pp. 9-10.

Chapter 13

CARE OF THE EARTH — A SPIRITUAL WAY OF LIFE

> *Our main task is to see that human technologies*
> *foster rather than destroy nature...*
> *our education needs to prepare us for that role...*
> *this is the spirituality of the future.*
>
> Thomas Berry[1]

> *The first aim of education should not be to*
> *prepare young people for careers but to enable*
> *them to develop respect for life.*
>
> Norman Cousins[2]

Perhaps more than any theories or discourse, the remarkable photo-graphs of the whole planet Earth, taken from space since the 1960's, show us the beauty, the oneness and the fragility of our planet. Almost every astronaut has been awed by the splendor of this view. James Irwin, who spent twelve days in space in 1971, commented, "The Earth reminded us of a Christmas tree ornament hanging in the blackness of space. As we got farther and farther away it diminished in size. Finally it shrank to the size of a marble, the most beautiful marble you can imagine. That beauti-ful, warm, living object looked so fragile, so delicate, that if you touched it with a finger it would crumble and fall apart."[3]

---

[1] Gerry Leonard, "An Interview With Thomas Berry," *NAMTA Journal*, Summer, 1991, p. 35-36.

[2] Ronald S. Miller, "Healing Ourselves, Healing the World, an Interview with Norman Cousins," *Peace in Action*, March/April 1986.

[3] Kevin W. Kelley, *The Home Planet*, p. 38.

It was only by leaving our planet and looking back at it, that human beings were at last able to appreciate the unique, but precarious, position of Earth in the solar system.

This view of our planet from outer space demonstrates with a new certainty the unity and interdependence of all the plant, animal and human life it supports. National borders that have caused so many wars and seem so important in political negotiations cannot even be seen in these photographs. Perhaps it is a preview of the next century when nationhood as we know it is likely to become obsolete. If the planet is to survive we may have to recognize nature rather than nation as our sovereignty. As the eminent paleontologist, Teilhard de Chardin, has said, "The Age of Nations is past. The task before us now, if we would not perish, is to shake off our ancient prejudices, and to build the earth."[4]

The photographs from space show Earth primarily in gorgeous blue and green hues that announce to the solar system that "Here we have life!" Here we have the blue of bounteous water and the green of lush foliage. Here we have the beauty of nature that has inspired countless artists, musicians and poets. In contrast, close-up photographs of other planets in our solar system show them to be barren and pock-marked. They have temperatures of either extreme hot or extreme cold and some are surrounded by gasses. None that have been studied so far support life of any kind, not even a tiny shrub. If something drastic should happen to planet Earth, there is no other sphere in our solar system that could offer life as we know it. Who would want to do anything to endanger the only home we have in space? It is shocking to realize how many of us are causing serious harm to our planet on almost every day of our lives.

Aldo Leopold (1887-1948), a truly great American naturalist, was one of the first to point out the necessity of a land ethic to insure that planet Earth would survive. "All ethics so far evolved rest upon a single premise: that the individual is a member of a community of interdependent parts...The land ethic simply enlarges the boundaries of the community to include soils, waters, plants, and animals, or collectively, the land.

"This sounds simple: do we not already sing our love for and obligation to the land of the free and the home of the brave? Yes, but just

---

[4] Pierre Teilhard de Chardin, *Building the Earth*, p.54

what and whom do we love? Certainly not the soil, which we are sending helter-skelter downriver. Certainly not the waters, which we assume have no function except to turn turbines, float barges, and carry off sewage. Certainly not the plants, of which we exterminate whole communities without batting an eye. Certainly not the animals, of which we have already extirpated many of the largest and most beautiful species. A land ethic ...affirms their right to existence, and, at least in spots, their continued existence in a natural state."[5]

Leopold wrote this plea for the land ethic before 1948; sadly, it has been heeded only by a small minority of the world population. Today, fifty years later, thoughtless people, motivated by profit and / or their own comfort, are causing even more drastic problems worldwide: many scientists feel that the ozone layer that shields the Earth from radiation is becoming depleted; acid rain is destroying large areas of plant life in the northern hemisphere; water pollution could continue to poison rivers and lakes and to put many specimens of aquatic life out of existence; some extreme deforestation is causing productive lands to become desert-like; lumbering in the rain forests is destroying the habitat of many species of plants and animals vital to our ecosystem; carbon dioxide and the heavy use of fossil fuels may be warming the surface of the earth, thereby threatening some melting of the polar ice cap; and affluent societies and industries are creating more waste than the planet can efficiently absorb.

A great deal of this destruction has occurred, I feel, because the natural world is not often perceived as conveying a spiritual presence. It has become a mere external object that can be dominated and manipulated by the will of human beings. One wonders how much healthier the condition of planet Earth would be today if more of our cultures had revered it during the last few centuries and considered its violation to be wrongful. I do not think that care of the earth was often promoted in sermons as a spiritual way of life, except perhaps by St. Francis of Assisi who could talk to the birds and named the celestial bodies Brother Sun and Sister Moon.

A look at indigenous cultures, however, shows us how love for the earth can be the intimate spirituality of daily living. Native Americans,

---

[4] Aido Leopold, *A Sand County Almanac*, p. 204.

for example, at the height of their culture were (and many still are) a very spiritual people. Traditionally the paramount characteristic of their lives was an intense interrelationship with their natural environment that constituted a behavior that could be termed a living spirituality. In their languages there is no word for *religion*. Their spirituality is an integral part of their lives that overflows into all their customs — hunting practices, respect for animals, reverence of the land, as well as into their sacred lore, ceremonies, crafts, dances, style of homes and relationships.

An explanation of this earth spirituality was given by the Navajo artist Carl Gorman: "We feel too insignificant to approach directly in prayer that Great Power that is incomprehensible to man. Nature feeds our soul's inspiration and so we approach the unknown power through [what] is close to us and within the reach of human understanding. We believe that this great unknown power is everywhere in creation. The various forms of creation have this spirit within them...As every form has some of the intelligent spirit of the Creator, we cannot but reverence all parts of the creation."[6]

There is a good reason why I believe that care of the earth is a spiritual way of life. When I ponder the four aspects of spirituality highlighted in Chapter 2, I feel that a careless attitude toward our planet violates each of these principles. It constitutes a lack of reverence for the earth; it ignores the possibility of a superior creative spirit in the universe; it exhibits arrogance rather than humility; and it defiles the sacred connection that each individual has with all of life.

David Hutchison, an alternative educator, writes, "The spirit is deeply rooted within an ecological context and seeks to establish the essential interdependency that exists among the organisms of the natural world...Therefore, within the context of a spiritual pedagogy, it is of paramount importance that the holistic educator instill (and sustain) respect for nature and its workings."[7]

Ideally a person who understands the process of nature will also understand the factors that endanger these processes and will join in the

---

[6] Carl N. Gorman, *The Indian Historian*, Winter, 1973.

[7] David Hutchison, "The Spiritual Realm within a Holistic Conception of Child Development and Education", *Holistic Education Review*, Fall, 1991, p. 20.

effort for responsible habitation of our planet. Because of the prominence of cosmic education in the Montessori curriculum, teachers and students are already quite aware of these ongoing processes. The challenge is to use this awareness to move both teachers and students to a passionate concern for the health of planet Earth — a concern that will be obvious, not just on Earth Day or recycle day, but in all their decisions, efforts and activities.

How can our overall vision of care of the earth come alive in our classrooms? To learn, children must do. "Individual activity," Montessori writes, "is the one factor that stimulates and produces development...this is not more true for the little ones...than it is for the junior, middle and upper school children."[8] Many ideas for Earth Care can be found in books and magazines. In addition I want to suggest some projects from teachers who are acutely aware of the fragile condition of our planet.

HELPING THE EARTH IN THE CLASSROOM

Connie Redwine, a Montessori teacher from Cincinnati, has designed a number of simple ecology lessons appropriate for ages 3 through 8. Her mission is simple: to help children understand that everyday activities have an impact on the ecological process of life. She wants to impart to children the necessity for using less fossil fuel energy, for using fewer materials, for making conservation a habit and for helping others do the same.

"In every classroom," she writes, "there is a morning routine. I urge you to incorporate into this daily routine a behavioral-awareness question, 'How did you help Mother Earth today? [or yesterday?]' Look for simple habits to emerge. 'I turned off the water while I brushed my teeth.' 'I drew on both sides of my paper.' 'I turned off the TV when no one was watching it.'"

Connie has put together a book[9] with many practical suggestions for classrooms. For example, after a discussion of acid rain, Connie suggests having the children water a plant with a mixture of 1/2 lemon juice and 1/2 water to show the adverse effects of acid rain on healthy

---

[8] Maria Montessori, *The Absorbent Mind*, p. 249.

[9] *16 Lessons for Our Planet*, which can be purchased from Connie S. Redwine, 4529 Mellwood Ave., Cincinnati, OH 45232.

leaves. Her book also describes some fun activities to demonstrate the effects of pesticides on the food chain that she calls the *Munch Line*.[10]

A WORM BOX

Many schools now have recycling and composting programs that help children to develop these habits at an early age. Judy Grove, a Montessori teacher at Penn-Mont Academy, tells of an indoor composting project — a worm box — that accommodates all the fruit and vegetable scraps in her classroom. Judy's father built the worm box according to the instructions in Mary Appelhoff's book — *Worms Eat My Garbage.*

"The children helped to shred the 9 lbs. of newspaper required for the bedding in the box. Then they placed the shredded paper in a large plastic garbage bag, and added enough water to produce an environment that was 75% moisture, the same as the worm's body.

"In December, we sprinkled 2 lbs. of red worms onto the bedding. I dug a hole in the bedding where the children could place their grape stems, apple cores, orange skins, banana peels etc. As the children met the worms on a daily basis, they delighted at finding baby worms and they were surprised at discovering what the worms love to eat best — cucumber.

"In the spring we harvested the vermicompost from the worm box, using a light that caused the worms to move quickly and totally away from one area of the box. This freed the newly made fertilizer to be taken from the box without removing the worms.

"We used the vermicompost on our outdoor gardens and on the plants that the children gave their grandparents in May. Watching the creation of this amazingly effective fertilizer was an experience we will never forget."

REDUCING WASTE

While recycling of waste is important, cutting down on the production of waste is even more vital. Habits of reusing materials rather than throwing them away can be started in every classroom. Here are some ideas suggested by several different teachers:

• Use cloth napkins rather than paper ones for lunches and snacks. Have the children wash their napkins as a Practical Life exercise.

---

[10] Adapted from *The Institute for Earth Education*, conceptual encounters by Sreve Van Marte, Warrenville, IL.

• Instead of bringing sandwiches in plastic baggies that are then discarded, bring them in a re-usable covered plastic container that can be washed and reused again and again.

• Use real cups and plates rather than paper ones. It is especially important to avoid styrofoam cups that cannot be recycled and take years to disintegrate.

• Ask children to remind their parents to reuse grocery bags or to have their own string bags that can be used over and over for transporting groceries.

• Ask parents for old letterheads or "used on one side" paper from their offices. The other side can be used in school and then recycled.

• Measure your classroom waste; see how much less it can be in a day or week.

HOW LONG TO DECOMPOSE?

To allow her students to see the consequences of throwing trash on the earth instead of recycling it, Judy Grove did a decomposition experiment in her classroom. She used a large glass window block that was half filled with soil. Into this container the children placed common items such as a small paper towel, pieces of plastic egg carton and paper egg carton, a wad of cotton, and a piece of plastic that holds a six-pack.

"We listed the items and dates; then watched for several months, occasionally adding water to simulate rain. We noted which materials disintegrated and which ones did not."

As a variation on Montessori's Time Line of History, Judy made a Time Line of Decomposition extending over 450 years. To do this exercise the children placed items on this Time Line according to the length of time it would take each particular item to decay if it were thrown on the earth. The following guide was used: piece of paper 2-4 weeks; cotton rag 1-5 months; rope 3-14 months; wool sock 1 year; bamboo stick 1-3 years; painted wooden board 13 years; tin can 100 years; aluminum can 200-500 years; plastic 6-pack cover 450 years; glass bottle, undetermined.

EARTH CARE REMINDERS

I suggest putting an attractive sign at each school entrance proclaiming, "This is an Earth Care Area." Like the signs "This is a Drug Free Area" that are now displayed near many schools, the Earth Care signs could remind children, teachers, parents and all visitors that here we are learning to care. We don't want pesticides, litter, styrofoam, plastic, excessive wrappings and wasted paper. Here we are making the Earth more beautiful.

Another daily reminder could be a special pledge of Allegiance. For many years this ritual has focused on national citizenship. The power of nations has been heralded but the preciousness of life has not been affirmed. For example, most countries have national anthems but there are no anthems for humanity. At this point in planetary history, without displacing our national allegiances, I feel, we must additionally recognize a more fundamental allegiance to the Earth and to the human family. With this in mind I have composed a new Pledge of Allegiance that could constantly remind children of this more spiritual commitment.

I pledge allegiance to the Earth
And to all life that it nourishes —
All growing things,
All species of animals
And all races of people.

I promise to protect all life on our planet,
To live in harmony with nature
And to share our resources justly,
So that all people can live with dignity,
In good health and in peace.

THE FUTURE OF PLANET EARTH

The children who surround us in the classroom are the adults of the future who will be making critical choices affecting the quality of our air, land, water, forests and wildlife. They will be voting for political candidates whose decisions will either damage or protect our environment. Now is the time to help our children to care passionately about what is happening to our planet. Such emotion, generated in childhood, can become a powerful motivation in later life.

"Even very young children care," Sister Anthonita Porta, Montessori teacher-trainer in Adrian, MI, pointed out in a lecture. "These are the years to nourish the habit of caring." Mary Truesdale reports that the three, four and five year-olds in her class began to cry when their butterfly emerged from the chrysalis. Because it was dripping with a reddish liquid, they thought it was wounded and bleeding. Karen Beerbower, an elementary Montessori teacher at Penn-Mont in Altoona, tells of taking ten elementary students on a four-day camping trip to an outdoor school where the instructors taught the children about the wild life that inhabited that special area. The final presentation was a skit put on by the instructors in which one of them posed as a particularly insensitive businessman who had come to buy the forest area for a housing development. He proposed cutting down all the trees, filling in the pond, clearing all the bushes. The children actually cried out in the middle of the skit, "No! No! You can't do that. Where would the owls go? What about the deer? And the groundhogs? And the ant hills?" It was the most emotional moment of the whole trip.

David Orr, Ph.D., a well-known conservationist, has a very frank message for teachers: "The survival of the planet depends on whether future generations can be educated in ecological literacy — an awareness of the interconnectedness of all life." He tells us we must be guided by the fact that "All education is environmental education. By what is included or excluded, emphasized or ignored, students learn that they are a part of or apart from the natural world."[11]   In almost all contacts with students we inculcate ideas of either careful stewardship of nature or passive acceptance of thoughtless habits that are cumulatively endangering the earth. Careful stewardship reflects a spiritual way of life. The spiritually-aware teacher can constantly reenforce this caring attitude with books, songs, ongoing projects, gentle reminders, and by displaying a large photograph of our planet Earth that was taken from space.

---

[11] David Orr, "Ecological Literacy," *Holistic Education Review*, Fall, 1989, p. 48-53.

Chapter 14

THE SPIRITUAL ROOTS OF PEACE EDUCATION

Preventing conflicts is the work of politics;
establishing peace is the work of education.

Maria Montessori[1]

When he received the Philadelphia Liberty Medal on July 4, 1994, Vaclav Havel, President of the Czech Republic, gave a memorable address on the crucial importance of a spiritual base for peaceful co-existence. President Havel said, "The only hope of people today is probably a renewal of our certainty that we are rooted in the earth and, at the same time, the cosmos. This awareness endows us with the capacity for self-transcendence.

"Politicians at international forums may reiterate a thousand times that the basis of the new world order must be universal respect for human rights, but it will mean nothing as long as this imperative does not derive from the respect for the miracle of Being, the miracle of the universe, the miracle of nature, the miracle of our own existence... It follows that, in today's multicultural world, the truly reliable path to peaceful co-existence and creative cooperation must start from what is at the root of all cultures and what lies infinitely deeper in human hearts and minds than political opinion, convictions, antipathies or sympathies: it must be rooted in self-transcendence."[2]

[1] Maria Montessori, *Education and Peace*, p. 27.

[2] *New York Times*, July 8, 1994, Op Ed page.

How closely this mirrors Montessori's message of 1949 — "We must develop the spiritual life of man and then organize humanity for peace."[3]

In other words, our efforts for peace cannot stand on their own, they must be rooted in spirituality. All the attempts of statesmen to draw peaceful boundary lines between nations and all the efforts of countries to build strong defenses against enemy attacks will not ultimately bring peace to the world. Peace will come only when people's hearts are imbued with respect for the Earth, for nature, for all other human beings, and when they can transcend personal gain to work cooperatively for universal good.

I have placed this discussion of peace after several other aspects of spirituality because I believe that the fostering of peace rests on stillness, wonder, respect for nature and the oneness of all people. For example, if we thoughtlessly dominate nature and use it recklessly for our own purposes, we may eventually use people in this same way. Anne Pattel-Gray makes this point very clearly in writing about the Aboriginal people. "We know that humanity's heart becomes hard when it is away from nature; we know that lack of respect for growing, living things soon leads to lack of respect for humans too. So we keep our youth close to softening influences."[4]

MONTESSORI AS A PEACEMAKER

The name, Montessori, has long been associated with the cause of peace. During the 1930's Maria Montessori spoke at major congresses in European cities, including Geneva, London, Brussels, Copenhagen and Utrecht. In many of these lectures she took an approach quite different from the other peace advocates of that time. Rather than dwelling on political solutions, she focused on the children who would be the men and women of the future. "If we ponder the influence that education can have on the attainment of world peace, it becomes clear that we must make the child and his education our primary concern."[5] For her innovative efforts over many years, Maria Montessori was twice nominated for the Nobel Peace Prize, in 1949 and in 1950.

[3] Maria Montessori, *Education and Peace*, pp. xii - xiii..

[4] Anne Pattel-Gray, *Through Aboriginal Eyes*, p.3.

[5] Maria Montessori, *Education and Peace*, p. 55.

"What is generally meant by the word peace," Montessori declared, "is the cessation of war. But...peace understood in this sense represents, rather, the ultimate and permanent triumph of war...the conquest of land and the consequent subjugation of entire peoples." Such actions sow the seeds for future conflicts. In contrast, "the prospect of true peace makes us turn our thoughts to the triumph of justice and love among men, to the building of a better world where harmony reigns."[6]

A peaceful atmosphere is usually associated with Montessori class-rooms. Visitors notice how comfortable the children are and frequently remark on the orderliness, beauty and serenity of the environment. This tranquility is not the result of tightly held reins; Montessori never equated good behavior with enforced silence and immobility. Children can move freely about the room and there is nearly always a busy hum of conversa-tion. The whole environment, however, is modulated by respect — respect for the teachers, respect for the children, respect for the materials and for all work in progress. This atmosphere, where cooperation rather than competition is encouraged, is fertile ground for peace education.

If such tranquility already exists in a Montessori classroom then why do we have further need of peace education? The answer lies in the fact that the environment alone does not give the children the skills of peace-making. These skills must be taught just as reading and math must be taught.

Colman McCarthy strongly advocates the teaching of peace at every level of education. "We are mostly peace illiterates, all but helpless to deal with conflicts. Is it imaginable that we would graduate students...without ever teaching them math and say, good luck, go muddle through? That's how we do it regarding conflicts: We graduate muddlers and then ask...why is America so violent?"[7]

It would be a wonderful tribute to Maria Montessori's long-stand-ing reputation as a peacemaker if Montessori schools in America would take the lead in giving children actual experience in peacemaking activi-ties. Quite a few Montessori teachers have already added such exercises

---

[6] Ibid, pp. 4 and 6.

[7] Coleman McCarthy, *"Peace Education: The Time is Now,"* The Washington Post, December 29, 1992.

to their classrooms—some of which I will describe in the next chapters. But for these exercises to be truly effective, each teacher must strive also to gain a sense of personal peace within himself or herself.

TEACHER'S PERSONAL PEACE

The teacher's integrity is a prime component. Ursula Thrush, a former Erdkinder[8] directress in San Francisco who is devoting great efforts to a required Peace Curriculum in all Montessori teacher training, says frankly, "We as adults must dare to take an honest look at our own values and attitudes. Are we preaching peace in the classroom and waging war at home? Are we, perhaps, open and loving toward our children, but envious of our colleagues? Are we cooperative with our immediate colleagues, but competitive with the personnel of other schools, or other branches of Montessori? If we are hypocritical in our own behavior, we cannot claim to be educators of peace. Our students learn not only from what we say but also from what we do and what we are."[9]

Sonnie McFarland, a Montessori teacher in Denver who has pioneered spiritual transformation for teachers of peace, also emphasizes the primacy of the teacher's role and the need to cultivate this role from his or her true spiritual center. "Our ability to call forth the peaceful spiritual nature in the children expands as we focus awareness on our own spiritual center of peace and develop sensitivity to the core of peace within the children. The more we come in touch with our spiritual center, the more we appreciate and respect the spiritual center of others."[10]

A peace retreat for teachers is an excellent means for teachers to build or restore inner serenity. Such an event enables them to withdraw for one or two days to a quiet environment and to nourish their spirits with nature, silence and sharing with others who are seeking the same kind of personal tranquility.

When I attended such a retreat for Montessori teachers in a beautiful secluded area of the Rocky Mountains, I was particularly inspired when we went into the woods in silence. We each found our own special place

[8] A unique educational experience devised by Maria Montessori for young teenagers.

[9] Ursula Thrush, *Peace 101*, p. 5.

[10] Sonnie McFarland, *Shining Through*, p. 1.

to sit, away from the others. Some of us simply drank in the beauty of that crisp sunny morning; some pondered; some prayed. Some of us reacted to the experience by writing a poem or making a meaningful drawing.

Sonnie McFarland, who with her husband, Jim, led the retreat, gave us the message clearly that, "In order to model peaceful behavior for the children, we must first have peace within ourselves." Her words were effective. After the retreat one of the Montessori teachers wrote to tell me, "In my personal life since our retreat two relationships of mine have been healed, one with my sister, after a 15 year estrangement, and one with a dear friend after a six year estrangement. I just wrote both of them from my heart and asked, 'Can we please have peace between us again?' They both wrote back and said 'Yes'. I guess I felt that if I was really going to work on peace, I should mend the hurts in my own life."

CHAPTER 15

CHILDREN'S INNER PEACE AND LOVE

If children, like adults, feel peace in their hearts, they can more easily relate peacefully to those around them. However, with so much stress and violence in our lives today, some children feel very little, if any, of this inner calm. Not all of the youngsters who come into our classrooms are secure and serene products of stable family situations. Over a million children each year see their parents divorced. They are relegated to one parent or they divide their time by days, weeks or seasons with one parent and then the other. Additional stress often occurs when either or both parents re-marry and the child must adjust to stepparents and, often, to stepbrothers and stepsisters. Other stresses arise from parents who are themselves tense and over-worked, from parents with drug or alcohol problems, from a variety of baby-sitters who may not relate well to children, from sibling rivalry, neighborhood bullies, racial tensions, and simply viewing the violence on the nightly news. Many frightening scenes are portrayed regularly on TV with little or no reassurance for children who may be watching.

These and other stresses bring us children who are disruptive, or who exhibit symptoms of withdrawal or who simply won't cooperate with classroom efforts. How can we help them? We can begin to heal their troubled spirits with centering exercises for the whole class preferably at the start of the school day.

REDUCING STRESS

Sheri Powell Coles, a teacher of second and third graders at the
Friends School in State College, PA, describes one way of doing this. "Our
daily centering begins with children sitting, lying down or standing
together. We close our eyes so that the outer world is shut out while we
focus on the inner. Breathing comfortably but purposefully helps to
focus us.

"Then we are ready to begin our inner voyage. One of the children's
favorite centering experiences is descending (in slow motion) flight after
flight of stairs from the top of a tall stone tower. After descending each
flight, we reach and pass by a door which we leave unopened. Finally,
after slowly walking down many flights, we reach the bottom door. We
slowly unlatch the door, and enter a room. We look around the room, and
stay there as long as we want. Finally, we leave the room and close the
door. We slowly and comfortably open our eyes and then anyone who
wants to share something from the experience is free to do so. The
children have shared their rooms in true wonderment. One child's room
was full of stars; another experienced an endless garden; yet another child
found himself enveloped in soothing colors."

Several Montessori teachers have told me that they use simple yoga
exercises to help children to feel inner peace. Holly Stoehr of the Kingsley
Montessori School in Boston reports having good success with the
postures described in the book, *Be a Frog, Be a Bird, Be a Tree.*[1] "I present
yoga to children with reverence and a certain amount of ceremony, e.g.
spreading a special 'Yoga Mat' onto the floor. Through creating both the
physical posture and sustaining the inner quiet, the children are engaged
in a process that involves their whole being. To an observer, the resulting
sense of peace and inner strength is almost tangible."

In a very thoughtful book, Clare Cherry describes games and
activities for stress reduction that she developed over a thirty year
period for children between the ages of two and eight. She writes, "If
children never learn how to turn inward they may be affected adversely
by unrelieved stress. It's not, however, simply a question of shutting off
the external world. I tell children to think of something quiet. I tell them

---

[1] Rachel Carr, *Be a Frog, Be a Bird, Be a Tree.*

to think of something inside themselves — to turn their eyes inward. The desired effect is to change their attention, however briefly, from the hectic, external world to the more peaceful world of mind and thought and fantasy."[2]

BUILDING SELF LOVE

Another factor that influences a child's inner peace is the way that he feels about himself. If a child does not like himself or feels that he is inferior to other children, he may use aggressive behavior to compensate for the perceived weakness.

In order to love others, all of us must first love ourselves. This self-love is not to be confused with selfishness which means over-concern with one's self without regard for others. A healthy self-love tells a child that she is a worthy person, unique in the universe, with special attributes and talents to contribute to the world. It does not say that she is better than anyone else.

To help children to be aware of their own self worth, Joanne Alex uses a "Magic Box." During circle she passes around a box with a hinged lid, telling the children that when each one looks inside he or she will see the most important person in the world. Each child opens the box carefully so no one else can look at the same time. What each one sees is a secret and can't be told to anyone else. Inside the box, of course, is a mirror that tells each child of his or her own importance.

Joanne also uses "Child of the Week" to emphasize, one at a time, the importance of each of her students. This is a display, changed weekly, featuring a large picture of one particular child, his or her favorite book, a favorite toy, hobby and perhaps a family photo and / or photo of a pet. On the last day of the week the child sits beside the display and Joanne reads from that child's favorite book, thus sharing with others something that is special to the Child of the Week.

When helping children to appreciate their self-worth and particular talents, it is wise to point out only their characteristics that have real significance. Lillian Katz, past president of the National Association for the Education of Young Children, warns against the shallowness of

---

[2] Clare Cherry, *Think of Something Quiet*, p. 4.

booklets like *All About Me* that ask the child to write, "What I Like To Eat," "What I Watch On TV," and "What I Want For Presents."

This booklet, like hundreds of others, puts the child in the role of consumer of food, entertainment and/or gifts. It has no page headings such as "What I Want To Learn," What I Am Curious About," "What I Like To Draw" or "How I Like To Help." Dr. Katz asks, "What are [the children] going to think when they discover just how trivial these criteria of specialness are?"[3]

Joanne Alex likes to acknowledge children who are helpful. She plays a game of "I Spy" in which the children guess which one of them she is referring to. "I spy someone who helped Takaki [a boy new to the class] today." "I spy someone who cleaned up the water on the floor." "I spy someone who introduced a visitor today."

Another contribution to a child's feeling of self worth is the use of his or her proper name by other children. A person's name is more than a label; it is a symbol of his or her essence. Usually a child is upset when called something other than his or her own name. Classroom ground rules usually preclude the use of any derogatory terms.

Midge Gallas, a Montessori teacher in La Grange, IL, tells of the children in her class making fun of a foreign child who had an unusual name that they found difficult to pronounce. To discourage this behavior without singling out the foreign child, Midge had the children do a project on the meaning of names. After the children researched the derivation of their first names, they took a new pride in them. Also they were surprised to learn that the name they had made fun of actually had a very noble meaning.

The birthday celebration commonly held in many Montessori schools affirms the child's place in space, time and cosmic reality. A candle is lighted to represent the sun and the birthday child carries the globe around the candle. The number of times she goes around the candle equals her age. If she is celebrating her fifth birthday, she encircles the candle five times, because the earth has made five revolutions around the sun since she was born.

---

[3] Lilian Katz, "Are We Confusing Self-Esteem and Narcissism? *Young Children,* November, 1993, p.2.

A beautiful book to read on a child's birthday is *On The Day You Were Born* by Debra Frasier. It places the child in the context of the whole cosmos and provokes gratitude for everything — sun, moon, stars, animals, fish etc. — that welcomed his or her new life.

GETTING IN TOUCH WITH INNER GOODNESS

Some teachers use *Starbright Meditations for Children* to help their students to use their imaginations to get in touch with their inner core of goodness. This is a lovely book of visualizations written by a mother of a young child. (When using it in a non-sectarian classroom, teachers must be selective because some of the visualizations are religiously oriented).

For these meditations the children sit or lie down with their eyes closed while the adult reads. The prelude begins, "I want you to see above your head a beautiful, beautiful star. This star is very special to you, as it is your very own star... It can be any color you choose...

"This special star is filled with lovely white light that shimmers and glows. I want you to see this light streaming down toward you until it reaches the very top of your head . . . Feel that light going (into) your body . . .

"I want you to...fill your heart with love for all the people and animals in the world...Can you see your heart getting bigger and bigger? It's expanding because you have so much love in your heart for all these people and animals, and of course for yourself."[4]

Such meditation and guided imagery help a child to become aware of his own spirit deep within himself. When his attention is frequently called to this interior self, he gradually realizes that within his body there is something very special. No one, not even the child himself can ever see this spirit but it can be reflected in his eyes, his smile and the things that he says and does.

Several teachers told me that they call this inner spirit the child's *lovelight* because it can be described as a warm feeling of love. Sonnie McFarland represents it with a lovelight candle — a votive candle that is almost completely covered by a beautiful spherical glass. When a child

---

[4] Maureen Garth, *Starbright Meditations for Children*, pp. 17-19.

needs time to think about some of her feelings, Sonnie takes the child to the Peace Corner in her classroom and lights the candle. The child can watch it burning and think about how her own light is shining or not shining within.

Cathy Heyliger, a Montessori teacher in Glenwood Springs, CO, calls this same inner spirit a *heartlight*. Cathy tells the children that each one's heartlight shines brightly when he or she has good feelings of love. It does not shine brightly when it is clouded over with feelings of anger, sadness, fear or jealousy.

She introduces the lovelight by reading them the book, *Something Special Within* by Betts Richter. "When I introduce this book to the children, I present it as one of my most treasured possessions. I tell the children that 'this book has a very special message for all of us to remember.' Because the book is somewhat lengthy, I read short segments at a time, usually to small groups. We then take time to talk about each of the ideas."

To symbolize the heartlight for the children, Cathy uses a flashlight with a heart outline glued inside it. The outline allows the light to shine through the heart shape. She also attaches a piece of velcro to the front rim of the flashlight. Then Cathy takes four squares of card stock and cuts out a heart shape in the center of each one. She glues a different colored piece of tissue paper on each square and puts a small piece of velcro on each of them.

To help her students to understand the heartlight, Cathy holds the flashlight against her chest, with the light pointing toward the children sitting around her in a dimly lighted room. Standing tall and confident with a beaming smile on her face she says, "This is how I look and how I feel when my heartlight is shining brightly." Then she dims the flashlight by using the velcro to attach one of the squares of colored tissue paper to it. With body language she portrays a negative feeling such as anger. "This is how my lovelight looks when I feel angry." Together they discuss what to do when you feel angry, so that you can help your lovelight to shine brightly again. Other feelings such as sadness, fear, jealousy, etc. can also be portrayed, each with a different colored square of tissue paper covering the flashlight.

The song, "This Little Light of Mine, I'm Going to Let it Shine," is very appropriate for any of the lovelight activities.

To help children become aware of the core of love that rests inside each one of them is, I feel, one of the most important aspects of nurturing spirituality and teaching peace. Whether you call this core the spirit, the real self, the lovelight, the heartlight or any other appropriate name does not matter. Use whatever term is comfortable for you in your situation. The important thing is to help the children realize that this special center of goodness is within them. This helps them to have a feeling of healthy self-love and to know that they have love to give to others. Montessori quotes the great Italian poet, Dante, as saying, "The greatest wisdom is first to love." She adds, "It is hoped that when this sentiment of love can be aroused in children, people in general will become more human, and brutal wars will come to an end."[5]

[5] Maria Montessori, *To Educate the Human Potential,* pp. 25-26.

CHAPTER 16

PEACE IN THE CLASSROOM COMMUNITY

It is interesting to see how little by little,
these [children] become aware of forming
a community which behaves as such...
Once they have reached this level, the children
no longer act thoughtlessly, but put the group
first and try to succeed for its benefit.

Maria Montessori[1]

Peace education is not only to be taught; it is most effective as an ongoing experience in the classroom community. Such a community values each member as a unique individual; it encompasses the habits of respect and fairness; it encourages the peaceful resolution of conflicts; and it gives each person a sense of belonging to a group whose combined efforts can be greater than that of any one member.

What does community mean in a classroom? Like a staff community, a classroom is a group of people who come together for a common purpose in a spirit of helpfulness and harmony. *Community*, I feel, is a very telling word to describe a Montessori classroom, and a very useful word to use frequently therein. The word *community* differs from the word *team*. In the world of sports, people on a team come together for a common purpose, but the purpose is always to beat or get ahead of an opposing team. Community, on the other hand, is not nourished by

---

[1] Maria Montessori, *The Absorbent Mind*, p. 232.

competition. Rather it is sustained by cooperation, mutual support and delight in each other's accomplishments.

WHO IS MISSING?

To affirm the importance of each person in her classroom community, Joan Gilbert designed an activity that invites a child to match an individual photo of each member of the class, including teachers, with that person's name printed on a card. Joan says it is one of the most frequently selected exercises in her language area. These photos can also be used as an activity for two or more children. One child arranges all the photos except one, in a circle, leaving a space for the missing picture. She then says, "Someone is missing from our community. Who is it? The other child or children must name the missing person and then return his or her picture to the circle. The game continues with children hiding their eyes while another child removes a different photo from the circle. The exercise shows that the presence of each person is necessary to make their community complete.

The circle itself is a wonderful symbol of community. It has no beginning or end, no front row or back row. Each sitting space is equal in rank, indicating that each person in the circle is equally important. The form of a circle has a long history of symbolizing togetherness. Many primitive cultures used it when drumming, chanting, and dancing, as well as for tribal meetings. Most Montessori classrooms have "circle" at least once a day. It is helpful, I think, to make the children aware of why this shape was chosen to gather everyone together.

THE MEDICINE WHEEL

For spiritual activities in her classroom community Sonnie McFarland uses the Medicine Wheel — a healing and harmonious symbol of relationships of life. Before introducing the material, Sonnie tells the children the story of Black Elk's vision.[2]

Over 100 years ago white settlers from the east were destroying the villages, the lands and the buffalo that the Native Americans in South Dakota depended on for food, clothing and shelter. Tragically the Oglala

---

[2] John G. Neihardt, *Black Elk Speaks.*

Sioux people saw all their culture and sustenance crumbling around them. One member of their tribe, a nine year-old boy name Black Elk, nearly died from a very serious illness. While he was in a coma he had a powerful vision that he did not reveal to anyone until many years later. "Black Elk," Sonnie continues, "beheld a circle that represented all of life — the four leggeds, the two leggeds, the wingeds, the creepy crawlies, the plants, the animals of the water, the sun, the moon, the stars and everything in the universe. He envisioned all of these to be of very great importance.

"He also saw four directions — North, South, East and West. He then noticed a Black Road of Difficulty running from east to west and a Red Road of Peace running from north to south. Where the two intersected, Black Elk beheld a sacred tree. When it was nurtured by kindness, this tree flowered and birds came to sing."

The Medicine Wheel can represent this vision in the classroom. Sonnie uses tape, white rope or braid, about 14 feet long, to form the all-encompassing circle on the floor. Then she adds a wide black ribbon or felt strip, about six feet long, stretching from east to west and a wide red ribbon or felt strip, of the same length, stretching from north to south. Where the two ribbons intersect, in the center of the circle, she places a small potted tree.

After the story has been told several times, Sonnie brings out a box of silk flowers, each one on a clip, and tells the children that whenever they do an act of kindness they can put a flower on the tree. When the tree is in full bloom, small replicas of birds are added to show that all nature rejoices in peace and kindness.

The Medicine Wheel, Sonnie feels, is a powerful metaphor that effectively symbolizes various aspects of behavior. For example if a child is misbehaving, the teacher can say, "You must be on the Black Road of Difficulty. Let me help you to get back on the Red Road of Peace." The silk flowers can be the focus of a discussion about kind acts that the children can do at home or in the classroom.

Judy Paulsen who has used the Medicine Wheel in her classroom for several years, keeps the little tree in a prominent place even after the rope for the Wheel and the ribbons for the Roads have been put away. "The tree is a constant reminder for the children to perform kind acts whenever opportunities arise." Judy removes the silk flowers and birds from the tree at the end of class every Friday. Then on Monday someone always says, "Wouldn't it be nice if we could make our tree bloom again this week?"

THE PEACE ROSE

Judy also uses a single silk flower, a rose in a vase, as a peace symbol for simple conflict resolution. Early in the year, at group time, Judy introduces this special way of working out difficulties.

"Two willing children pretend that they are having a problem and are about to have a fight. One of them (or a third child acting as a mediator) gets the peace rose. While holding the rose, one of the involved children can speak, telling what happened and how he feels about it — 'I was very mad when you took the pieces out of my puzzle.' He may not call names or be verbally abusive, such as saying, 'I hate you.' (We have previously worked on this with role-playing that demonstrates how to express one's feelings without being hurtful. 'I' messages are best for this, such as, 'I felt sad because you wouldn't play with me.')

"Then the other child holds the rose and expresses her feelings to the first participant. When the two children reach a solution or simply get over their difficulty, they (and the mediator if there is one) put their hands on the stem of the rose and say, 'We declare peace.'

"Once the children have learned this procedure it becomes the routine means of conflict resolution in which the teacher is never involved. All staff must be consistent in this procedure. When any child asks a teacher to referee a disagreement, the standard response is 'Do you think you need to get the peace rose and take turns talking?'

"We have used this simple method for four years now," Judy says, "and it is incredibly effective. We keep one rose in the classroom and a second one on the playground. One of the greatest advantages is that the peace rose allows the teacher to remain withdrawn from any fracas. That alone defuses any attention-getting fight. Also it unhooks the teacher from all the traps of tattle tales, and relieves her of the burden of having to decide who was in the wrong. The great bonus is that children learn to recognize feelings — their own and others'— while practicing skills to handle conflict. Many of our parents have told me that they now keep a peace rose at home."

USING VINYL BALLS FOR FEELINGS

Another creative means to help children deal with feelings was suggested to me by Debbie Wolf who with Elaine Bosse founded the classroom program, "Choices for Peace Making," in Columbus, OH. "Vinyl balls, each labeled with an emotion, are playfully thrown to the students to use as the concrete representations of the abstract concept of emotions. The students "catch" *afraid, angry, frustrated, crabby, nasty, joyful, mean, sad, peaceful, lonely, happy, stubborn, embarrassed, silly, etc.* Then the balls are used to show how the students can make choices as clearly and simply about their feelings as they can about the balls they have caught. 'What can you do with the ball you are holding?' They give a variety of replies — 'Throw it, hide it, share it, hit somebody with it, pack it away, forget about it, play with it, put it away until tomorrow or throw it away.' We respond, 'It is the same with your feelings. You always have choices about your feelings and what you do with them.' "The students are taught that their feelings are okay and real. Children are not responsible for the feelings they have, but they are responsible for what they do with them. When they realize that they can deliberately choose a peaceful response, children feel a new sense of control — 'I don't have a choice if someone hurls anger at me, as they might hurl a ball, but I do have a choice about whether or not I become angry in response.' This new awareness makes a strong case for kindness and peaceful behavior."

BRIDGES OUT OF WALLS

Judy Paulsen suggests another peace activity that involves singing. Using a set of large blocks, two willing children build a wall between themselves, while their classmates watch. On opposite sides of the completed wall they stand with their backs toward the wall, pretending to be mad at each other. As the group begins singing the song *Building Bridges Out of Walls*,[4] the two children take down the wall, and with the same blocks, they build a bridge. Then they hold hands and walk across the bridge.

---

[4] Helene and Dave Van Manen from their cassette, "Healthy, People, Healthy Planet."

Although discouraging negative behavior is a vital element in creating a peaceful community, it takes more to do the job. Peace does not automatically occur when conflicts are eliminated. All of us need daily reminders —books, posters, symbols, pictures, songs, poems, stories, games, dances — to work for peace. Something as simple as a mirror hanging at a child's height near the classroom door, Rebecca Janke suggests, can be such a stimulus if it has a sign on it that says, "Peace begins with me."

VIRTUES

One of the four aspects of spirituality that I highlighted in Chapter 2 was that "spirituality summons us to the highest of human virtues, such as love, caring, generosity, responsibility for our actions, forgiveness, compassion and openness to one another. It leads us to sharing rather than accumulating, to cooperation rather than competition and to peace rather than violence."

Certainly the classroom community is a fertile environment for cultivating virtues. I do not mean studying them in the abstract, such as devoting one week to honesty and the next week to truthfulness. I mean acquiring virtues in the daily give and take of the classroom community. "It is only in the community that man's potentialities can be realized," Montessori observed. Like Dewey she believed that, "Morals are connected with actualities of existence, not with ideals... The facts upon which [morals] depend are those which arise out of active connections of human beings with one another."[5]

Perhaps the basic principle to be emphasized in a classroom community is the Golden Rule that is common to all the major religions as I noted in Chapter 3. This maxim urges all of us to treat others as we want to be treated. As such it covers all the virtues. One can say to a child who has taken another child's property, "Would you want Alisha to take your new pencil?" "Would you want Jeffrey to say that he didn't take your cookies when you saw him eating them?" "Would you want every-one to laugh at you when you fell down?" "How would you like it if no

---

[5] John Dewey, Human Nature and Conduct; an Introduction to Social Psychology, p. 329.

one let you play with them?"   "If no one shared their candy with you?" Helping children to feel as others feel is a touchstone that can easily be used to nourish the spiritual virtues.

THE GOOD HEART JOURNAL

There are many books, songs and programs on the market that support the teaching of peace. For example, Rebecca Janke, a Montessori teacher in Minnesota and Julie Peterson have formed an organization called "Growing Communities for Peace." Among the many suggestions in their teacher's guide they recommend keeping a Good Heart Journal in any classroom community to help children focus on positive qualities. This is a beautifully covered three-ring binder containing descriptions and drawings of good deeds.

"We bring this book to our closing ceremony each day. When the children gather, we ask them what peace-making behavior they saw or did that was helpful, kind, caring or loving. If the children are non-writers the teacher records the deed and the child makes a little drawing... We keep this book accessible at all times. The children find it fascinating because it represents our community's life together."[6]

WORKING TOGETHER

In a classroom community it is particularly important to let children experience the joy of creating something together —something that would not be possible for one child to do alone. In many classrooms children join together to form a chorus, to put on a play, to do group dancing or to build a structure. In each instance the spiritually-aware teacher will remind them that these activities are possible only because everyone in the community participates. Several teachers have told me of other such projects — children cooperating to paint a large mural on the wall in the school yard; children working together to make a patchwork quilt with each child designing and sewing one of the patches; children making a Time Line of Peacemakers with each student telling about one man or woman who worked for peace;[7] and the classroom community

---

[6] Rebecca Janke and Julie Peterson, *Peacemaker's A,B,C's, for Young Children*, p. 19.

[7] Ruth Fletcher, *Teaching Peace*, p. 59.

combining pennies, nickels and dimes to save enough to buy an acre of rain forest that will, because of their combined effort, be saved from destruction.

Joanne Alex describes a hand quilt that her students made. "First each child found a shade of construction paper that matched her skin. On this paper, each child traced her hand, cut it out, and glued the hand on to a square of paper. Each child decorated her square and printed her name on the palm of the hand. When they had all finished we arranged the squares on a large piece of colored poster-board so that it looked like a patchwork quilt. While doing this we talked about how each one's square helped to make our quilt unique and beautiful. No other group of children could make one exactly like ours."

"What would classrooms be like," Mara Sapon-Shevin, Associate Professor of Elementary and Special Education at the University of North Dakota, asks, "and how would children interact ...[if] love and caring were considered not just acceptable behavior, but central organizing values?...One teacher I know places her students in little clusters of desks pushed together.

"She calls these groups *families,* and she has a basic rule in her classroom: If anyone in a family group has a problem (of any kind), it is up to the group to try to solve it before coming to her for advice or help. The nature of the problem goes beyond not knowing what math page to do...She has seen these families of children rally around a child who was sad, upset or worried about something — little heads buzzed together as they figured out what to do to help."[8]

GIVING VOICE TO PEACE

To reenforce their experience of peacemaking and problem solving in the classroom community, it is important for children to verbalize it in some way. Noreen Kerrigan Cadieux, a Montessorian from Delmar, NY, says, "In our classroom we regularly use a universal recitation for peace

---

[8] Mara Sapon-Shevin, *"Schools as Communities of Love and Caring,"* Holistic Education Review, Summer 1990, p.24.

that was taught by one of Gandhi's nephews. The children make accompanying gestures as they chant:

> *I offer you peace;*
>
> *I offer you love;*
>
> *I offer you friendship;*
>
> *I hear your cry;*
>
> *I see your beauty;*
>
> *I feel your pain;*
>
> *My wisdom flows from my spirit within;*
>
> *I salute that spirit in you.*
>
> *Let us work together for peace."*

CHAPTER 17

THE SCHOOL AS A FAMILY/GLOBAL COMMUNITY

Goodness must come out of reciprocal
helpfulness, from the unity derived
from spiritual cohesion.

Maria Montessori[1]

For more than thirty years I have visited Montessori schools through-out the United States as well as in a number of other countries. It has always seemed to me that the most comfortable schools with the least number of financial or administrative crises were those that functioned in very close association with the families of their students. Here it was obvious that staff and parents knew each other well and were confident of the others' good intentions and expertise. Therefore both were tolerant when human failings occurred. In other words, parents were not quick to withdraw their children at the first sign of trouble and teachers did not easily give up on students with unusual problems. They worked together to help each child.

I like to think of such a school as a family of families or a spiritual community. With so many young families today living long distances from their own extended families, the school community can offer them a welcoming place to belong. Here they can meet other parents with simi-lar aspirations for their children; here they can talk over their mutual

---

[1] Maria Montessori, *The Absorbent Mind*, p. 242.

concerns and here they can absorb Montessori's principles of parenting while participating in various school projects. It is not only the parents who appreciate this family type community. The staff, too, constantly feel a special kind of support and they do not hesitate to ask for parent help when it is needed.

INVOLVING PARENTS

The assistance they ask for usually goes beyond making cookies for a school event. In such a Montessori community parents are often asked to share more of themselves — their professions, skills, hobbies, talents, customs, native languages etc. — and to take a more active part in their children's education. For example, a mother who is a laboratory technician may bring in a microscope and show children how to examine pond water; a father who is a carpenter may work with some children to build a bench or a gate for the school yard.

Betsy Hoke always involves parents in star observing — an activity that can take place only at night. She keeps a Star Bag in her classroom containing a flashlight, a chart of the constellations and a Star Journal. Each child has a turn to take the Star Bag home.

First, the child and parent(s) study the sky chart for that particular time of the year in their locality. Then on a clear night they go out together to observe the constellations, using the flashlight to refer to the chart. After returning home the child, with parent help, notes their observations in the Star Journal. The child then shares his experience at school the following day.

Parents can also participate in other nature experiences — hikes in state forests or overnight camping trips. In a community-type school parents do more than drive a car or carry the first-aid box. They attend preparation sessions such as those when a forest ranger comes to the school to tell the children what to look for on an upcoming hike. They learn how to help the children discover the treasures of nature in a particular area; they learn to respect the silence of the forest and to feel awe and wonder as the children experience it. Parents who participate in such activities are often inspired to take hikes or camping trips with their own children at a later date.

This triad of children, teachers and families is the foundation of the highly successful schools in Reggio Emilia in northern Italy. The city-run educational system originated in schools started by parents, schools that they literally built with their own hands at the end of World War II. Loris Malaguzzi, who from the start has guided and directed the energies of both parents and educators in Reggio Emilia, says, "To think of a dyad of only a teacher and a child is to create an artificial world that does not reflect reality...

"We strive to create an amiable school where children, teachers and families feel a sense of well being; therefore the organization of the schools — contents, functions, procedures, motivations and interests — is designed to bring together the three central protagonists — children, teachers and parents —and to intensify the interrelationships among them."[2]

USING THE 102 GREAT IDEAS

Carmen LaFranzo, head of Carmel Montessori Academy (for ages 3 to 18) in Warrenville, IL, places the parents firmly in the role of raising the level of their children's education. This can be done, she feels, by changing the focus of daily family conversations from mundane subjects to discussions of some of life's most thought-provoking concepts, such as Truth, Justice, Change, Happiness, Democracy, etc., based on Mortimer Adler's list of 102 Great Ideas from the Great Books of the Western World. Each year the children, their families and the faculty at Carmel consider thirty-four aspects of the Great Ideas — approximately one per week. Carmen believes that "not even three year-olds are too young to participate if we structure our questions and discussions to meet their developmental level."

Carmen's weekly news sheet, typed by her elementary classes, contains questions on each week's topic that can be discussed by all age levels at family meals or while riding in the car. For example, on the topic of "Animals: Beings Between Plants and Men" she suggests the following:

Toddler / Pre-primary

Stories of the close and mutually beneficial relationship between animals and human beings are a good way to begin discussion of animals with the very young child.

---

[2] Loris Malaguzzi, "For an Education Based on Relationships," *Young Children*, November, 1993, p.9.

Primary

> What part do animals play in our daily lives?
> What makes a pet different from any other animal?
> How are our friends different from our pets?
> How do the places where animals live affect their lives,
> their behavior, their relationship to human beings?

Elementary

> How do animals differ significantly from human beings?
> In what ways are they the same?

Erdkinder

> What is there in our intelligence that we do not see in the
> operations of animals? Discuss personification and allegory
> regarding animals as they reveal the human condition.

The give and take on these truly great ideas nearly always touches on spiritual considerations. Because all families in the school are participating, their discussions usually overflow into further conversations with peers and teachers.

APPRECIATING DIFFERENT CULTURES

A typical class of American children may be in reality a microcosm of the global community. Therefore it is a natural setting for expanding children's awareness of multicultural traditions. Nearly all the children have parents, grandparents, or other ancestors who came to the United States from different parts of the world. Students can research their ancestral background perhaps by interviewing the oldest living member of their family. Then they can present this family story in class with family pictures and objects of particular interest. Some children's parents who were born in other countries may be willing to tell the class about their customs, crafts, holidays, games, etc., and perhaps serve samples of their native foods. Sharing like this helps everyone develop respect for all nationalities and cultures.

There are many other ways that families can help the school to become a global community. Through their contacts with friends and relatives abroad, families can recruit pen pals or sister schools in foreign countries. A different language is not necessarily a barrier; children can communicate with drawings, photographs and especially videos of each other's schools featuring the children learning, playing, singing and dancing. Several months after a little boy who had been in Stillwater Montessori School in Maine returned with his family to a Montessori school in Tokyo, each school made a lovely book of photographs showing their daily routines. Explanations and comments were in both languages. There was great excitement when the American book arrived in Japan and when the book about the Japanese school arrived in Maine. It was truly a multicultural project based on personal experience.

LEARNING ABOUT INJUSTICE

Many teachers have told me of activities that they use to make children aware of the injustice in our global community — injustice that, until it is addressed, will always threaten world peace. The book, *Teaching Peace*,[3] has several interesting charts that illustrate various types of injustice. One shows clearly how 20% of the world's population uses 80% of the world's resources. This can be translated into a class of 20 children with a supply of 20 pencils. Most children will say that each child should have one pencil. But if the pencils are divided according to the chart of world resources, four children receive 16 pencils, or four pencils apiece. The other 16 children have only 4 pencils or 1 pencil for every four children. The injustice of this becomes clear if the teacher asks the class to do a timed writing project. The 16 children with only four pencils will be at an unfair advantage; they'll be frustrated and may become aggressive and try to use some of the extra pencils that the other four children have.

Another concrete example of world conditions is a chart showing a large percentage of the world population living on a small percentage of the world's land. To demonstrate this, the classroom can be divided into world land areas according to the chart on page 95 of *Teaching Peace*. Then the student population, divided proportionately according to the same chart, can move their desks into their assigned space. The most crowded and frustrated group will be those representing South Asia which has 50% of the world population living on 16% of the world's land.

---

[3] Ruth Fletcher, *Teaching Peace*.

Some Montessori schools, with parents assisting, serve a world population dinner every year to elementary age students. A few children are given a full dinner including soup and dessert, complete with attractive plates, chairs, table and tablecloth. A larger number of children have beans, rice, fruit and milk served in cracked or chipped dishes on bare tables. Finally the largest number of children equal to the other two groups combined eat a small bowl of rice with a little milk as they sit on a straw mat or large leaf on the ground. A more detailed menu for preparing a World Lunch can be found on page 96 of *Teaching Peace*.

To reach out to a third world country, Carmel Montessori Academy adopted a school in Sierra Leone to which it regularly sends school supplies. These American students have developed a personal caring relationship for this African school that has constant need of basic materials that our students usually take for granted.

CELEBRATIONS

Community in its fullest sense calls for celebration. Since the beginning of history every culture has honored its values and traditions with various kinds of periodic rituals. A school community that has worked together for a common purpose can also pause to recognize its unity of spirit, recent accomplishments, multicultural diversity and/or efforts for peace. Like other joyful celebrations these rituals can include singing, dancing, reciting, sharing food and symbolically portraying their oneness of purpose.

DEDICATING A PEACE POLE

One outdoor celebration that I particularly like is the dedication of a Peace Pole in a prominent location on school grounds. A Peace Pole is a handcrafted wooden obelisk that stands seven feet tall when it is 'planted.' The message, "May Peace Prevail on Earth," is inscribed in four different languages, one on each of the four sides of the obelisk. Schools may choose any four languages from the 37 that are available. These include, among others, Korean, Hindu, Russian, Hebrew, Spanish, French, Japanese, Chinese, English and American Sign Languages.[4]

---

[4] For information write to the Peace Pole Makers, 3534 W. Lanham Road, Maple City, MI 49664

Each community planting a Peace Pole can design its own dedication. At Montessori schools the children often carry the small flags from
the different countries of the world. Some children and their families
wear native costumes and/or play native musical instruments. The
community is reminded that war begins with thoughts of war, and peace
begins with thoughts of peace. The celebration usually concludes with
the singing of peace songs and/or a universal prayer for peace.

Over 100,000 Peace Poles have been planted in 100 countries around
the world since 1955. They serve as constant reminders for people everywhere to visualize and work for world peace.

HARVESTFEST

"Our school environment has been and will continue to be the
natural place for community to grow," says Michelle Hartye, head of Penn-
Mont Academy. "This is very evident in our yearly Harvestfest celebration in mid-October."

This year 60 parents participated in the all-morning celebration of
the Harvest — an event at Penn-Mont that has replaced the annual
Halloween party. The teachers set up special activities in their classrooms
as well as in the school yard. Each parent was in charge of taking three or
four children around to all of the activities. The youngest children
particularly enjoyed a harvest hunt. A small plastic swimming pool was
filled with wood shavings under which were hidden small pumpkins,
Indian corn, various kinds of squash, apples and pears. Each child could
reach in and harvest a piece of fruit or a vegetable. Other activities
included making scarecrows, tasting a variety of apples, making leaf
rubbings and leaf prints, cider-making, harvest dancing, sampling
harvest treats like pumpkin squares and apple cake; donating food for
the local food bank; and riding bikes around a path for donations to St.
Jude's hospital. At the end of the morning everyone gathered in a
tremendous circle in the school yard. Over 250 people held hands and
performed a harvest dance. "Together we gave thanks for our community —for the children, the parents, the teachers and for planet Earth that
had so generously given us our wonderful harvest."

WINTER SOLSTICE

Another time of year that lends itself to community celebration is the winter solstice in the third week of December — the darkest week of the entire year. Because the days are so short during this period, people from many different cultures and religions have traditionally held celebrations of light. Here I shall describe one that is based on an idea from Sonnie McFarland.

Sonnie invites parents of various cultural and religious backgrounds to explain their traditions to the children in her school in the weeks prior to the winter solstice. An example of this is the Jewish celebration of Chanukah starting on the first night with one candle representing one night's worth of oil. It ends eight nights later with the other eight candles burning in the menorah because the one night of Biblical oil miraculously lasted for eight nights. Other examples are the Christian preparation for Christmas using the one rose colored and three purple colored candles of the Advent Wreath representing the four weeks of Advent that precede Christmas and the African-American celebration of Kwanzaa (December 26 to January 1) using three red candles, three green candles and one black candle each representing a principle or belief.

If other cultures are represented in the student body their celebrations are also explained. These might include the Swedish celebration of St. Lucia's Day; the Hindu festival of lights called Divali; the Latin American celebration of Las Posadas; the Orthodox Catholic celebration of Epiphany.

On the night of the community celebration Sonnie puts a Medicine Wheel (described in Chapter 16) on the floor of a large room. In the center of the Medicine Wheel she places a lighted lovelight candle. The rest of the room is in darkness. As the families arrive, each person is given an unlighted taper. When the ceremony begins a Jewish parent places a menorah in one segment of the Medicine Wheel, lights the candles and explains the tradition. Then a Christian parent places the Advent wreath in another segment of the circle, lights the four candles and describes their meaning in preparing for Christmas. The other traditions are then demonstrated in the same way. After each presentation the room becomes visibly brighter showing that each religious tradition adds light to our lives.

Then the head of school lights a taper from the lovelight and begins to sing, "One lights another," as she lights the taper of the person next to her. The song continues "One lights another, One lights another, One lights another until the whole world is one." As each person's taper is lit he or she joins in the singing. When the last taper is lighted the chorus is full and the room is brilliant with light. Then everyone sings "Let there be peace on earth and let it begin with me."

A community relationship that can be celebrated in this way is usually one that has matured over time in an atmosphere of openness and acceptance. Such a community is nourished by supportive acts of kindness — one parent driving for another who is ill; one family sending a casserole when another family has a new baby; families helping teachers in the time crunch before the first day of school; teachers giving extra time when it is needed and many other gestures of mutual support. As each individual feels respected and valued by others in the community, all gradually become comfortable in this family-like atmosphere that serves as a paradigm for our wider participation in the global community.

"The key to community," Scott Peck writes, "is the acceptance — in fact the celebration — of our individual and cultural differences. Such acceptance and celebration...is also the key to world peace."[5]

[5] M. Scott Peck, *A Different Drum*, p. 187.

Chapter 18

SPIRITUALITY AND THE ARTS

We should help the child...because
he is endowed with great creative energies,
which are of a nature so fragile
as to need a loving and intelligent defense.
Maria Montessori[1]

The creative energy of a child is an outward expression of his or her spirit. As a unique attribute, unlike that of any other person, this energy must be protected, nourished and never forced into conformity. Pablo Picasso once said (in an unknown source), "Every child is an artist. The problem is how to remain an artist once he grows up." It is vital, therefore, for Montessori teachers, who are called to nurture the spirit of each child, to provide a fertile setting for the creative expression of this spirit in art, music, poetry, drama and dance.

Unfortunately these are the subjects that are often the first to be eliminated (particularly in public schools) when budgets are cut. Administrators often consider them to be curriculum frills because of being unaware of their intrinsic value to the development of the whole child. Confronting this attitude, John Frohnmayer, former chairman of the National Endowment for the Arts said, "There is no question in my mind that a person who has been educated in the arts is going to have a better

---

[1] Maria Montessori, *The Absorbent Mind*, p. 28.

understanding of the world generally. People in the arts learn to self-evaluate and to take risks, and those are the characteristics of a good thinker."[2]

Abraham Maslow makes this point even more strongly. "Creative art education may be especially important, not so much for turning out artists or art products, as for turning out better people...If we hope for our children that they will become full human beings, and that they will move toward actualizing the potentialities that they have, then the only kind of education that has...such goals is art education."[3]

When nurturing artistic expression we should first give particular attention to Montessori's call for a "loving and intelligent defense" of the child's great creative energies." Like Montessori, Joseph Chilton Pearce, author of *Magical Child* and *Evolution's End*, emphasizes the fragility of these powers. After many years of studying the intelligence of growing children, Pearce, like Steiner, classified the early years as the sensitive period for developing creative imagination — the human power ultimately responsible for our great inventions, explorations, scientific breakthroughs and artistic compositions. It is a time when imaginative play greatly stimulates this power within the child.

Television, Pearce believes, deadens creativity. "There are sixteen acts of violence per hour of children's programming," he writes, but "the major damage of television, has little to do with content: Its damage is neurological...Television floods the infant-child brain with images at the very time his or her brain is supposed to learn to make images from within."[4] Storytelling, on the other hand, stimulates the creation of corresponding internal images. This imaging is the foundation of future symbolic thought, mathematics, science, philosophy, etc. Children who constantly watch TV gradually weaken this vital ability. The inadequacy begins to show on the playground.

As I talked to teachers while preparing this manuscript, many voiced their concern about the lack of imagination in children's play. Instead of making up games or pretending, many children at play time simply mimic scenes they have seen on TV. When they act out TV scenes, they are

[2] "Frohnmayer Visit Prompts Arts and Ethics Discussion," *Crescendo*, Winter, 1995.

[3] Abraham Maslow, *The Farther Reaches of Human Nature*, p. 57.

[4] Joseph Chilton Pearce, *Evolution's End*, pp. 164 and 169.

copying someone else's creations and leaving their own powers of imagination unused. If we are to protect children's creative energies that express their own unique spirits, we must make parents aware of this serious effect of TV watching.

MONTESSORI AND THE ARTS

Montessori was well aware of the spiritual character of artistic expression. "When there are found in the caves of primitive men those surprising coloured drawings of animals in movement, they tell us that artistic genius for drawing existed from the time of the origin of man; but these fine representations were not merely a way of finding expression or of communicating pleasing ideas, but are generally supposed to stand for religious ideas."[5]

Noting that the arts, like the intellect and spirit, make humans unique among living beings, she wrote, "Every human group loves music...Let us think what this means; none of the animals have music and dancing, but the whole of mankind, in all parts of the world, knows and makes up dances and songs."[6]

Montessori took particular interest in the hand as the instrument of man's creative energies. "All men will resemble one another in the way they use their feet. But no one can tell what any given man will do with his hands...The hand is in direct connection with man's soul...and in the light of history we see it connected with the development of civilization...If men had used only speech to communicate their thought, no traces would remain of past generations...When a free spirit exists, it has to materialize itself in some form of work, and for this the hands are needed. Everywhere we find traces of men's handiwork, and through these we catch a glimpse of his spirit."[7]

Montessori incorporated training of the child's hand in the Casa Dei Bambini with many manipulative materials. For example, she provided metal insets to trace multiple geometric shapes and colored pencils to fill in these shapes with a variety of hues. This activity she considered an

---

[5] Maria Montessori, *The Discovery of the Child*, p. 347.

[6] Maria Montessori, *The Absorbent Mind*, p. 120.

[7] Ibid, pp. 148-151.

essential preparation for both handwriting and drawing, so that the child's hand would function with precision when performing these skills at a later time.

Nearly all Montessori classrooms today include many materials for creative expression such as crayons, modeling clay, an easel and paints. These art supplies are usually in the child's regular classroom, rather than in a separate art room, so that they are always available as a choice of individual activity. Art activities often help to relieve stress in children. Joanne Alex suggests using warm play-dough for a centering activity for children who have just come in from outdoors on a cold day.

HAIKU

For a lovely experience in creative writing, Linda Alston, a Montessori teacher at Maria Mitchell School in Denver, encourages her five year-olds to compose haiku, the beloved poetry of the Japanese. A haiku consists of three lines which contain five, seven and five syllables respectively. "To this requirement," Linda writes, "add three others: the haiku should contain some reference to nature; it should deal with a particular occurrence; and what is going on in the poem should be in the process of happening." Her example:

Tiny water bead
rolls over the soft green leaf
refusing to pop.

The study of haiku is particularly appropriate in a spirit-filled classroom because it invokes a very peaceful response. "Haiku," Linda believes, "holds within it the power to transform. It is a wake-up call from the earth to its children to come, commune with it, and experience its beauty."[8]

MUSIC

According to Linda Thompson, of the Rochester Montessori School in Minnesota, the methods of the famous Japanese music teacher, Shinichi Suzuki, are quite congenial with those of Montessori. Both held a deep

---

[8] Linda Alston, "Teaching Haiku to Young Children," *The NAMTA Journal*, Spring, 1993, pp. 43-50.

respect for children, encouraged non-competitive activities and advocated matching ability to interest, isolating difficulties and doing repetitive exercises. Like Montessori, Suzuki adhered to the *second* definition of education — to bring out, to develop from latent or potential existence, rather than the *first* definition — to instruct. Both emphasized the importance of the environment. Suzuki feels that talent is inborn and that everyone has talent. "But," he stresses, "talent must be nurtured by the environment."[9]

I will never forget an example I once witnessed of a group of six to nine year-old Montessori children who had absorbed music from the environment. I went to observe a class one afternoon right after lunch. All the children were working at individual activities. As I watched, I gradually became aware that they were humming a classical melody. Later when I asked about it, the teacher, Mary Claire FitzGibbon, said "Oh yes, that's the second movement of a Brahms Symphony. I usually play it as background music in the afternoon but today I forgot to turn it on."

REPRODUCTIONS OF FINE ART

Hanging reproductions of fine art in the environment also enables children to absorb details of some of the world's great cultural treasures. When we opened our Montessori school in 1961 I hung a beautiful print of Picasso's *Child With a Dove* on the classroom door — not at the usual five feet above the floor, but way down at the eye level of the children. That painting, I thought, seemed to announce to anyone coming into the classroom that "this is a peaceful place." I had intended to hang a different print there every month but amid all the busyness of that first year I forgot to change the display. In May an eight year-old painted an amazing copy of this painting without having it in front of her. She had truly absorbed all the details as she opened the door of her classroom every morning.

"Among the pictures in our Children's Houses in Rome," Montessori wrote, "we have a copy of Raphael's *Madonna della Seggiola*...The children, of course, cannot comprehend the symbolic significance of the *Madonna*

---

[9] Linda K. Thompson, "Montessori and Suzuki, *The NAMTA Journal*, Spring, 1990, pp. 43-49.

of the Chair, but they will see something more beautiful than that which they feel in more ordinary pictures."[10] Montessori recognized that little ones could relate in their own way to a masterpiece. This insight is confirmed by modern research: after reviewing many available studies, Feeney and Moravcik concluded that "the early years appear to be the optimal time to lay the foundation for a lifetime of enjoyment of the arts."[11]

Fine art has always been a "Don't touch" subject for young children, thus depriving them of their most natural means of learning. My own published program of *Child-Size Masterpieces* has changed this approach in many pre-schools and elementary classrooms. By matching, pairing, sorting and sequencing postcard-size reproductions of famous paintings children can absorb their details, note similarities in several paintings by one artist, learn names of famous painters, compare schools of art and observe art history on a time line.[12]

When children come into contact with an art masterpiece (or reproduction thereof), it is a far deeper experience for them than looking at a cute little commercial image. In fine art they meet an expression of the artist's spirit. Like Montessori, I believe that children can sense when something is more worthy of observation, "something more beautiful than that which they see in ordinary pictures."

MEDITATION AND CREATIVITY

Teacher Stephanie Herzog tells how the daily meditations she does with the children in her class stimulate the creative flow in their artistic activities. Because so many beautiful images emerge from the children's verbal sharing after meditations, she feels it is an ideal time for them to express these images in either drawing or writing, "to bring out and express on paper their private inner song."

"Meditation" she writes, "allows children to calm the normal chatter of the mind and tune to another part of themselves, that part wherein lies true imagination and true spontaneous creativity...Vibrant

---

[10] Maria Montessori, *The Montessori Method*, pp. 82-83.

[11] S. Feeney and E. Moravicik, "A Thing of Beauty: Aesthetic Development in Young Children, *Young Children*, September, 1987, pp. 7-15.

[12] Aline Wolf, *Child-Size Masterpieces*.

images of feelings lead to vibrant colors on the page, and children stretch their minds to come up with the words that can clothe their inner experiences...I no longer have to provide a subject or prod them to think of ideas."[13]

JOY

Joy is one of the great gifts of the spirit. While spiritual nurture always includes periods of quiet and solitude it must also frequently erupt in expressions of joy. Singing, dancing, painting, pretending, constructing, playing with puppets, imagining characters while listening to a story are all expressions of children's joy. I particularly feel the human spirit in the exuberance of song and dance. Why not dance more with children? Not necessarily formal dancing, just moving spontaneously to the rhythm of beautiful music. What else says so clearly that it is good to be alive? Dancing and all the other arts allow children to express their inner spirituality with the joy that is such a natural element of childhood.

[13] Stephanie Herzog, *Joy in the Classroom*, pp. 127-129.

CHAPTER 19

CONTROLLING ADVERTISING IN THE ENVIRONMENT

The immense influence that education can
exert through children, has the environment
for its instrument, for the child absorbs
his environment, takes everything from it,
and incarnates it in himself.

Maria Montessori[1]

When Montessori teachers think of preparing the environment they usually have an image of painting shelves and buying materials which when arranged carefully will invite children to perform various learning tasks. Some teachers, particularly sensitive to noise, think of putting carpet in certain areas of the classroom. Others, concerned with nurturing spirituality think of 'peace corners' and displays of nature. All of the preceding are vital to the prime importance that Montessori gives to the environment; but they are not the totality. Every person in the classroom, as well as the clothes worn, the sounds made, the objects carried in, are all part of the environment that is absorbed. To keep our environment consistent with Montessori ideals requires constant vigilance. If we are trying to create a space where children's spirits can thrive, we must attempt to shut out the clutter of the commercial world.

I recently visited a school in California where no child was allowed to come to school with a jacket, T-shirt, lunch box or notebook that

[1] Maria Montessori, *The Absorbent Mind*, p. 66.

displayed a violent or ugly scene or that advertised a trade name, TV character or movie. What a welcome change it was to see clothes that were not
screaming with commercials. Several students had made their own
designs for their T-shirts —designs that indicated what was important to
them rather than what was important for a corporation to advertise.

Why should we allow our children to provide free advertising for
corporations that care nothing about the quality of a child's life? Classrooms, even Montessori classrooms, where children wear Batman capes
and Power Ranger gloves have lost their essential tranquility. Such
gimmicks not only reinforce the idea that we must buy all the latest fads,
they also prompt behavior that is associated with these products — often
of a peculiar or violent nature. Children need advocates who can say a
firm "No" to blatant commercialism.

ANALYZING ADVERTISING

It is wise for Montessori parents and teachers who are serious about
spiritual values to take a critical look, not only at clothing, but at all the
advertising in today's culture. Much of this incessant selling is aimed
directly at children, who are victims of its seemingly unlimited power.
According to *Consumer Report*, businesses and trade associations target
no less than 30,000 commercial messages at children every day on TV,
radio and billboards. Many thousands more are emblazoned on school
buses, posters, study sheets, workbooks, audio visuals and clothing.

Selling to children is big business. Today's elementary-age children
have tremendous spending power. In total they spend $11 billion per
year on a variety of products from food, beverages and clothes to toys
and games. In addition, they influence another $160 billion of spending
controlled by their parents. One Madison Avenue advertising agency
blatantly brags it can put its client's product in kindergarten lesson plans
and can help develop product loyalty by distributing samples to elementary students.[2] According to Joseph Chilton Pearce, "Psychologists have
determined that, given the right inputs and programming, by six years of
age a child's buying habits can be determined for life."[3]

---

[2] *Captive Kids*, A Report on Commercial Pressures on Kids at School, Consumer Union Education Services, Yonkers, NY, 1995.

[3] Joseph Chilton Pearce, *Evolutions' End*, p. 195.

Advertising is developed by professionals — many of them psychologists — who know how to manipulate children's desires. Children have no defense, no experience that has taught them to resist. They beg and whine to have clothes clearly marked with a brand name and they constantly pester for toys advertised on TV. "When they identify with the television children playing with the same toy," says Joseph Chilton Pearce, "they feel some group authenticity, a sense of belonging not found elsewhere. Television, of course, is the way to sell those toys that then represent the television images that are flooding the young brain, reinforcing the television stimulus when that stimulus is absent."[4]

Advertising not only teaches children to want inferior products or products that pollute the environment (such as toys that repeatedly require batteries or that are made of plastic); it teaches them consumerism as a way of life.

Children need to be trained to analyze advertising. In elementary classes, I suggest discussions that would deal with how they can be lured into unwise decisions by TV commercials. Examples of questions to ask are: "Is it a good idea to buy a particular brand of sneakers because some well-known athlete is paid several million dollars to wear them? What about the quality, the fit, the durability and the price?"

"Is it wise to buy a soft drink because a TV ad for it shows a professional athlete making a spectacular ski jump? Does this image imply that you can ski like this if you drink the same cola? What about the sugar and caffeine in the drink? What does it do to your body? Is it habit forming? What about its packaging — the aluminum can and the plastic six-pack holder that take over 400 years to decompose?

"Do you know that multi-million dollar production studios have tricked you into providing hundreds of dollars worth of advertising for their movies and TV shows when you wear T-shirts featuring gaudy images of the characters they have created? Do you know that when you buy that T-shirt you are paying them to let you advertise for them?" The book *Teaching Peace* features specific activities to help children to analyze and resist such commercials.

---

[4] Ibid, p. 169.

Our economy is based on the premise that there is a potential market for almost any item we can produce, regardless of its intrinsic value, effect on the environment, planned obsolescence, or the fact that no one may really need it. Advertising is the vehicle that introduces this item to potential buyers. It often creates discontent by making consumers feel inadequate or socially unacceptable if they don't have it. Paul L. Wachtel writes, "I do think that advertising stirs desires that might otherwise not be there, and often to our detriment. But it does not write its message on a blank slate... Growth, progress, the idea of 'more' is so much a part of our consciousness that it takes very little to persuade us that any particular item is something we want or need."[5]

It is hard to reconcile this state of mind with a more spiritual outlook that is considerate of the needs of unfortunate people. Advertising and its resultant consumerism crowd out the spiritual approach to life. It favors manufactured products over the gifts of nature. It frequently disregards environmental issues. It usually promotes selfishness and acquisitiveness over sharing and kindness. It values passive entertainment rather than self-directed or inner-directed activities. It tells people subtly, "You can have everything, even if others have nothing."

For these reasons I feel that we must help children to evaluate advertising and recognize its power over our decisions. We must free our environments from its unrestrained influence so that we can nurture the spiritual rather than materialistic aspect of the young children in our care.

---

[5] Paul L. Wachtel, *The Poverty of Affluence*, p. 18.

Chapter 20

WHAT ABOUT GOD?

Some teachers in non-sectarian schools feel uncomfortable with children's questions that touch on the transcendent. They often seem at a loss when children ask, "Where does God live?" "What happens to people when they die?" "Why did God let my daddy's car get in a crash?" or "Who made the world?" These are children's versions of the perennial questions of humankind. Most of us pursue them for a lifetime.

The Spiritual Life of Children quotes Dorothy Day, the peace activist who devoted much of her life to the poor, as saying, "I remember all the wondering I did, all the questions I had about life and God and the purpose of things...Some of the things I asked then — asked my parents, my friends and a lot of times myself — I'm still asking myself now forty or fifty or sixty years later."[1]

Instead of setting aside such questions with responses like "I think you should ask your parents," or "We'll talk about that some other time," questions like these should be honored as audible signs of children's developing spirituality. "That's a very good question, Nicky" or "I have often wondered about that myself," is a good response with which to start.

To help adults deal with questions from children who come from widely differing religious backgrounds, it may be helpful to consider the

---

[1] Robert Coles, *The Spiritual Life of Children*, p. 329.

concept of God from the historical viewpoint. The idea of God (or the gods of the Greeks, Romans, Hindus and others) has intrigued and mystified human beings since the dawn of civilization.

In *A History of God*, Karen Armstrong, writes, "Men and women started to worship gods as soon as they became recognizably human; they created religions at the same time as they created works of art. This was not simply because they wanted to propitiate powerful forces; these early faiths expressed the wonder and mystery that seem always to have been an essential component of the human experience."

The word *God* has always meant something slightly different to each group of people who have used it in various periods of history. "The statement 'I believe in God,'" Armstrong asserts, "has no objective meaning, as such, but like any other statement only means something in context, when proclaimed by a particular community...The same is true of atheism. The statement 'I do not believe in God' has meant something slightly different in each period of history...Had the notion of God not had this flexibility," she believes, "it would not have survived to become one of the great ideas."

The long history of the concept of God affirms that men and women throughout the ages have experienced a spiritual dimension that goes beyond the everyday world. "This human experience of transcendence has been a fact of life," Armstrong declares. "Not everybody would regard it as divine: Buddhists would deny that their visions and insights are derived from a supernatural source... All major religions, however, would agree that it is impossible to describe this transcendence in normal conceptual language." Monotheists have called this transcendence *God*, but the use of this term has certain religious restrictions. Orthodox Jews, for example, when using the vernacular, refrained from writing or properly pronouncing the numerous Hebrew names for God found in sacred texts. Muslims must not attempt to depict the divine in visual imagery. These disciplines are reminders that the concept we call 'God' exceeds all human expression.[2]

---

[2] Karen Armstrong, *A History of God, pp. xix-xx and xxi.*

In modern western religions God is sometimes referred to as He, but in many earlier civilizations, the supreme deity was a goddess. Joseph Campbell, like many other scholars, believes that God is neither male nor female. "It's absurd to speak of God as of either this sex or that sex," he says. The divine power preceded the division of life into two different sexes.[3] Despite this probability, children frequently picture God as an old man up in the sky. Often they try to ascribe human characteristics to God because such attributes are within their familiar frame of reference.

The teacher who struggles with children's questions about God is not alone in searching for answers. Any discussion of God labors under impossible difficulties. Joseph Campbell says that this is because "God is an ambiguous word in our language...It appears to refer to something that is known. But the transcendent is unknowable and unknown."[4] For many people God becomes significant in their lives, not through factual knowledge, but through religious faith and the scriptures.

Because the word God is sacred to many people, I feel children should not use it casually or carelessly, such as saying "Oh God," or "Oh my God" when one is surprised or struggling. Teachers can help children to refrain from such profanity which is often offensive to those who hold the name of God in reverence.

We should not be surprised when children talk about God. It is a word that is in most children's vocabulary — a word they have heard at home as well as in places of worship. And it is a word that undoubtedly will enter our non-sectarian classrooms. How should we handle it? With respect, with understanding, and with honesty.

RESPECTING THE QUESTION

When a question about God arises a teacher in a non-sectarian setting must be keenly aware that the surrounding children may come from atheistic or agnostic backgrounds or more probably from a variety of religious faiths. Some may have strong beliefs in God, in Allah, in

---

[3] Joseph Campbell with Bill Moyers, *The Power of Myth*, pp. 49-50.

[4] Ibid, pp. 48-49.

Yahweh, in Jesus. In responding, it is best to show a deep respect for these beliefs or unbeliefs without giving priority to any one persuasion.

"My mom said that Jesus saved me so I can go to heaven," a six year-old announced recently at circle time. "I'm glad you told us that," the teacher replied, affirming the child without confirming or denying his statement.

When a child asks if God made the world, a response might be, "Some people think that God made the world and other people do not think that God made the world. It's a question that people have been trying to answer for thousands of years. I am glad you are thinking about it, too."

In fact we should never feel that we have to come up with a definitive answer to a question like "Are we ever going to see God?" or "Can God see what we are doing?" Admitting that you don't know, along with many parents or many brilliant scholars, is an honest reply that may lead to further discussion or to insights from the child himself. Robert Coles records such a conversation with nine year-old Tommy who was trying to draw a picture of God:

Tommy asked Coles, "Isn't it a big secret, what He looks like?"

"Yes, I think so."

"Do you think He looks like us?"

"I don't know."

"I don't think He does. He might look real different."

"Like what?"

"Oh," said Tommy, "like something that doesn't even exist here."[5] Professor Coles, by admitting that he didn't know, had made room for a very profound thought from a child.

On the other hand, a teacher with a strong religious faith in God may feel it is dishonest to reply, "I don't know" when a child asks, "Do you think God is for real?" Such a teacher may feel that he or she "knows" that God exists but also realizes that he or she cannot teach this belief in a non-sectarian setting. What kind of reply will not violate his or her personal integrity? It must be very honest such as, "I have never seen

---

[5] Robert Coles, P. 60.

God but I believe God exists. Many people believe that God is real and many other people do not believe that there is a real God. It is a big question for each of us to think about".

UNDERSTANDING THE QUESTION

When faced with a deep question from a very young child we sometimes have to stop and ask ourselves "What is she really asking?" Jean Grasso Fitzpatrick says, "When a three year-old asks, 'Why did God make the flood come?' after hearing the story of Noah, he is not grappling in the abstract with the problem of evil. He is looking for reassurance that his home — and Mommy and Daddy and his brother and his precious toys — are not going to end up under water."[6]

Children who see floods and other disasters on TV, often harbor a dreaded fear that they, too, are about to become victims of such catastrophes. Teachers can look for such fears in unusual questions and give a comforting reply — "We don't live near a river so it is not likely that our homes will be flooded." Or if the school is located in a threatening area, "Don't worry about being hurt in a flood. We always get warnings before the water overflows, so you will have plenty of time to go to a safe place."

"Why did God let Poppa Jack die?" is a kind of question that might be brought to a teacher. When a child asks about someone else's death he is probably expressing some fear that he, too, is going to die. Therefore our answers to children's questions about death should be age-appropriate and as reassuring as possible. Reassurance, however, must be honest. If a child asks directly, "Am I going to die?" it is neither truthful not helpful to say, "Of course not (meaning not soon)." It is harder but more honest to reply, "We all have to die, but most people die when they are very old after they have lived a long life."

RETURNING THE QUESTION

Perhaps the most important consideration for a teacher to focus on is "How can I respond in a way that will continue to nourish the child's spiritual growth?" Often this is done by returning the question to the child to encourage him to ponder it. "Where is God?" a child may ask. "That is a question that each of us can think about. Where do you think God is?"

"I think God is up in the sky," a child might reply. And this answer may spark a variety of ideas from other children:

"Maybe God is the sun watching us."

"God might be in a fire, like the burning bush."

"My Dad says, 'God is in the church.'"

"Maybe God is right here but we can't see Him."

Children's questions and comments about God force us to reflect on our own beliefs; they stimulate our spiritual growth even when we have no answers, even if we have no faith.

One of Joseph Campbell's favorite stories was about a troubled woman who came to the Indian saint and sage Ramakrishna, saying, "O Master, I do not find that I love God."

And he asked, "Is there nothing then that you love?"

To this she answered, "My little nephew."

And he said to her, "There is your love and service to God, in your love and service to that child." [7]

Chapter 21

EXPLAINING SPIRITUAL NURTURE TO PARENTS

One reason that the spiritual element of Montessori education is not more frequently emphasized is that it is usually difficult to explain it to parents. Teachers and heads of schools, who are not always clear about this spiritual element in their own minds, often have trouble putting it into words for parents of prospective students. And because the parents have not been made clearly aware of it, teachers sometimes feel uncomfortable in giving the *spirit* the priority it deserves.

It may be helpful here to look at how this problem is handled by the Friends Schools that are based on the ideals of the Quakers. These schools usually have a large constituency — both staff and students — of non-Quakers. No effort is made to convert the non-Quakers to Quakerism but all who are concerned with a Friends school know that its underlying philosophy includes Quaker values.

For example, the head of a Friends School told me that when parents come in to register a child he tells them that Quakers believe that "there is that of God in everyone." This basic value is the inspiration for fostering character development that includes respect for all other human beings, — other races and cultures as well as for the unfortunate and oppressed. Such respect leads to the cultivation of simplicity, peacefulness, caring and other virtues.

If parents are not comfortable with this philosophy, this head of school suggests in a gentle and supportive manner that they enroll their child elsewhere. However, in his many years of administration only a very few have chosen to do so. Furthermore, he said, this openness with the parents has freed the staff from any hesitation about encouraging Quaker values.

I believe that now is the time for Montessorians to take a new pride in the spiritual element of our educational values. We can tell parents that underlying all our academic programs and efforts to help children to become independent, to concentrate, to observe with all their senses and to form good working habits is Montessori's highest aspiration of nurturing the spirit of each child.

Essential to this message is the distinction between nurturing the spirit and teaching a particular religion, as explained in Chapter 3. Nurturing the spirit, we can explain to parents, will include experience of silence and reflection, a reverence for nature, an appreciation of the interconnectedness of all things, and the cultivation of peacefulness, compassion, generosity and love. If prospective parents are troubled by this overall emphasis on the child's spirit, they might wish to choose another type of education for their child or children.

But this frank explanation is not likely to drive parents away. I believe they will appreciate the spiritual emphasis as a trend whose time has come. Given the current interest in spirituality described in Chapter 7 and the dismay which many parents are experiencing with the violence, dishonesty and crass materialism of our culture, they may welcome a renewed emphasis on spirituality. In an age when the major educational alternatives seem to be sterile secularism on the one hand or education that serves a particular religion on the other, Montessori and other holistic schools can offer parents the ideal compromise — an enriched academic program with a spiritual depth.

The world needs such a favorable combination in educational philosophy. We should be proud that our founder's highest aspiration was to bring about a better world through nurturing the spiritual growth of children.

Afterword

THE "END" TO KEEP IN MIND

How can we as spiritually aware teachers, a relatively small group of adults, work effectively in a culture that seems to be rushing headlong away from the values of stillness, wonder, simplicity, peace, compassion and care of the earth? Is such an effort asking too much of teachers and teacher trainers who are already overburdened with academic work? Montessori, herself, realized the enormity of this task: "It is true that education can create a better kind of man but this is a vast undertaking. It is a labor that may well take a long time, but it will nonetheless be brief in comparison to the work that man has already accomplished."[1]

"The starting point for a better world," the late Norman Cousins said, "is the belief that it is possible... The wild dream is the first step to reality. It is the direction-finder by which people locate higher goals and discern their highest selves. If our purposes are frail, if our concern for the next generation is uninspired, if the value we attach to the idea of progress is small, then we'll bow before the difficulty. But if we have some feeling for the gift of life and its uniqueness, if we have confidence in freedom, growth, and the miracle of vital change, then difficulty loses its power to intimidate."[2]

---

[1] Maria Montessori, *Education and Peace*, p. 80.

[2] Ronald S. Miller, "Healing Ourselves, Healing the World — an Interview with Norman Cousins," *Peace in Action*, March/April, 1986.

To locate the higher goals that he speaks of, we must constantly search for the essence of Montessori's work. If we were to read through all her writings and lectures we would find, I think, that she used many more words pleading for the nourishing of "an entirely new child whose astonishing characteristics can eventually contribute to the betterment of the world," than she used for academic presentations. To this point she spoke frankly: "In going about his dedicated labors in behalf of the child, the adult must realize above all else that his task concerns a revelation of the child's soul. If he does so, the steps he subsequently takes and the aid he offers the child will be of great importance; if he does not do so, all his work will go for nothing."[3]

By quoting this I do not mean to undermine the importance of the Montessori classroom materials. I have always thought that they are ingenious. They invite the child to learn with her hands, elucidate difficult concepts, lengthen his span of concentration, encourage independence, allow the child to follow her own interests. But in the sum total of Montessori's life they were not her first priority; they are a means, not the end.

In his widely praised book, *The 7 Habits of Highly Effective People*, Steven Covey tells of the significance of Habit #2 — "Begin with the End in Mind." "It's incredibly easy," he says, "to get caught up in an activity trap, in the busyness of life, to work harder and harder at climbing the ladder of success only to find it's leaning against the wrong wall...

"How different our lives are when we really know what is deeply important to us, and, keeping that picture in mind, we manage ourselves each day to be and to do what really matters most."[4]

What is "the end to keep in mind" for Montessori teachers? I believe it is the kind of adults our students will eventually become. Will they be men and women who, no matter what path they choose to follow in life, will be guided by spiritual strengths that were encouraged in the Montessori environment of their childhood?

Great teachers, I believe, carry with them a larger vision of the purpose of a class than the goal of any particular lesson. They look not

---

[3] Maria Montessori, *Education and Peace*, p. 91.

[4] Steven Covey, *The 7 Habits of Highly Effective People*, p. 98.

only at the child in front of them but at the adult emerging from these sensitive years. In daily interactions they hope to foster men and women who know deep down that there is more to life than what they observe with their senses, who pause to appreciate the wonder of the universe and who honor its ineffable questions, who feel a deep reverence for the Earth and all living beings, who believe that life is filled with meaning and are optimistic about the future, who have the courage to voice their inner convictions and to live by them, who are able to rise above self-interest and self-gratification to take some significant steps for the good of humanity, who cherish peace within themselves and strive for peace in their relationships and for peace in the world.

It is my hope that many Montessori graduates will be guided by these strengths which are more likely to develop when we give priority to nurturing spirituality in our classroom communities. Such personhood was Maria Montessori's most cherished goal. It deserves to be the "end" we keep in mind.

Appendix

A DISCUSSION OF RELIGIOUS EDUCATION

Although any child's inborn spirituality can be nurtured by the ideas and activities presented in Part Three of this book, there are many Montessorians who believe that non-sectarian spirituality is not enough. These individuals - who may be parents and/or teachers - are convinced that the full flowering of spirituality can occur only when it culminates in a belief in a Supreme Being, expressed in a particular religious faith.

As an advocate of Christian religious formation for young children, Sofia Cavalletti, a Catholic, believes that Maria Montessori's work reaches its highest point when children are, in some way, helped to know God. "To want to stay on a level of religiousness deprived of content would be tantamount, as Santayana stated, to wanting to speak a language without using a spoken tongue. If we intend to talk about God we must use a language, and the language with which we speak of God takes the name of an actual religion."[1]

Other educators feel strongly that no religious beliefs should be handed automatically to a child who has not yet wrestled with the ultimate questions or asked for the answers that religions offer. G.I. Gurdjieff, philosopher and explorer of the sacred traditions of both east and west, advised, "One should always begin from afar in such a way that [children's] own search would be encouraged. What we do with children should be a response to their search."[2]

Sanford Jones, a well-known Montessorian, believes that it is not wise to wait for such questions; children need the security of being reared in one particular religious tradition. "I have increasingly less patience with parents who say, 'I feel my child should grow up open-minded, so I'm going to wait until he is old enough to choose for himself.' What parent would allow the child such choice in the areas of language or mathematics?"[3]

---

[1] Sofia Cavalletti, *The Religious Potential of the Child*, p. 27.

[2] J. G. Bennett, *The Spiritual Hunger of the Modern Child*, p. 71-72.

[3] Quoted by Carol Dittberner, "The Pure Wonder of Young Lives," *The NAMTA Journal*, Fall-Winter 1987, p. 82.

Several generations ago children were almost automatically reared in the religious tradition of their families. Most still are. But today, parents — especially those who have drifted from their own childhood faith or who are in a marriage of mixed religions — do not always instinctively make this choice for their children. Rather, they hesitate to commit their family to one specific faith. "Because it is such a hard thing for some people to deal with," says Jean Kunhardt, a developmental psychologist who is a partner in a Jewish-Christian marriage, "many simply...do nothing. And they end up losing out on some things they might really benefit from as a family."[4]

Whether or not to introduce children to a specific religion — at home, at school or at a place of worship — is a question that is rarely considered at Montessori parent meetings. And yet, I feel, it is a question that burns, sometimes painfully, in the hearts of many mothers and fathers. Could it not be discussed in an objective way, perhaps by a panel of parents and teachers? An airing of this topic could help those who are wrestling with a difficult decision about religious education.

Parents who hesitate to make religion a vital part of their children's lives often cite reasons from their own upbringing: they feel they were brainwashed; they feel they were led to think they were superior to followers of other religions; they feel that what they learned in Sunday school was irrelevant or totally imbued with fear and guilt; they feel religious leaders are too authoritative and dogmatic, etc.

Because such issues are emotionally charged, these parents have not been able to look uncritically at what religion may mean to young children. For example, religion can give a child a sense of identity — of belonging to a community that celebrates and supports the major transitions in life with baby-naming ceremonies, Baptism, Bar and Bat-Mitzvahs, Confirmation for adolescents; marriage rituals and burial rites.

Religion can give children a sense of security that may be particularly helpful amid the tension and violence in today's society. For example, children may feel protection in the belief that God loves them or that they have a guardian angel who constantly watches over them.

---

[4] Martha Fay, *Do Children Need Religion?* p. 15.

Children may find comfort in religion when they are faced with an accident, serious illness, the death or departure of a loved one or any other serious disturbance in their lives. Religious beliefs may be able to sustain them or try to give them answers at such difficult times.

Religion also makes children aware of their own goodness. "We give our children a sense of their worthiness in many ways," Rabbi David Wolpe writes. "None of those ways is more important than reminding them that they are created in the image of God. Being created in God's image makes a person invaluable. As adults we can see God's image in the faces of these new lives... entrusted to us."[5]

Religion can support parents in working toward one of their most cherished goals — that their children will be good people. As parents consciously or unconsciously model moral and virtuous behavior, religious instruction can reenforce it. It is a voice for ethical, respectful and compassionate living in what is often an insensitive and self-serving culture.

Parents who want their children to have a religious faith must decide whether to give these children religious instruction at home or to take them to church, temple or mosque. If they decide to take them to a place of worship, I believe that they have the right to insist that their religious institution, no matter what denomination, provide a positive experience for children that is developmentally appropriate. An overly dogmatic program, with little regard for the child's level of maturity or readiness, can be negative and even spiritually detrimental. Criticizing the religious education of her time that focused heavily on sin, Maria Montessori warned, "To speak of evil to the small child is to teach him something which he is not capable of understanding, or at least which he cannot assimilate. Great prudence is therefore required in the teacher, so that she may not hurt the soul of the child with arguments ill-suited to his nature."[6]

"The main aspect of the religious life of the child," Carol Dittberner, a teacher-trainer, writes, "is, and should be joy! ...Young children need to be told over and over again that they are loved: They are loved by their

[5] Rabbi David J. Wolpe, *Teaching Your Children About God, A Modern Approach.*

[6] Maria Montessori, *The Discovery of the Child*, p. 363.

parents, and they are loved by God. The prophetic announcements, 'Be joyful! Do not fear! God is near!' are the proclamations for childhood."[7]

I have met Montessori teachers whose classrooms are in schools that are actually part of religious institutions. Using Montessori methodology and philosophy, these teachers have beautifully integrated the religious dimension of their programs into their Montessori classroom environments. One such teacher is Noa Goldman whose pre-school class is in Ner Tamid — a Jewish Synagogue in Baltimore.

Most Jewish children are introduced to their religious traditions in their homes, particularly at the weekly celebration on the eve of the Sabbath and the special family rituals held at home for Jewish holidays, such as Passover, Rosh Hashannah, Yom Kippur and Chanukah.

Noa explained that she anticipates the weekly Sabbath meal by having the children perform the traditional rituals in the classroom first — as a preparation that will help them to better understand and participate in the celebration in their homes.

Children take turns playing the role of Abba, the father, and Imma, the mother. The make-believe mother covers her hair and lights the two Sabbath candles to begin the ceremony. Then the make-believe father blesses the miniature challah — special Sabbath bread — and grape juice, used here for the children instead of the usual wine.

On Thursdays Noa tells the story of that week's Torah portion to the children, or talks about an ethical or moral idea from that portion relevant to the children. They also sing Jewish songs about God — joyful songs that indicate He is everywhere and loves everyone.

For parents who have chosen a Christian affiliated school for their children, there is available a more extensive and formally developed religious education program that also proclaims love and joy. Based on cultivating the mysterious bond between God and the child, Sofia Cavalletti's *Catechesis of the Good Shepherd* brings Montessori principles and techniques to religious education for children. Her program, which is age appropriate for 3-6, 6-9 and 9-12, involves sensory learning, manipulative materials and child-size objects all based on religious tradi-

---

[7] Carol Dittberner, op. cit., p. 84

tions. With a true Montessori perspective, she has matched key spiritual content with the corresponding sensitive periods.

The *Catechesis of the Good Shepherd* was designed for teaching Christianity. However, many of the ideas and techniques could be adapted for other religions, particularly those that incorporate sacred stories and ritual objects.

Because I believe that the *Catechesis of the Good Shepherd* is an example of a very appropriate program for children, I want to make it known to any readers who are seeking meaningful Christian religious education for their children. Therefore, I have asked Catherine Maresca, a teacher trainer for *Catechesis of the Good Shepherd*, to describe this program in more detail in this Appendix.

THE CATECHESIS OF THE GOOD SHEPHERD
by
Catherine Maresca

Throughout history, the human spirit has reached for God. The world's great faiths, expressed in word, art and architecture, testify to this movement of our spirit. At the same time, these expressions of faith actually support our spiritual life, drawing our senses, our minds, and our hearts towards God. While all of creation is a revelation of God, enjoyed and contemplated by people of every faith, more particular revelations of God serve as the foundations of the world's religions.

Introducing children to the faith or religion of their culture or family is an important part of their spiritual development. It complements exercises such as those in Part Three of this book, which nurture the spirit in a non-sectarian manner. Because of its importance, such an introduction should be as carefully considered as every other material in a Montessori environment.

We have all seen "seasoned" children in a Montessori classroom move peacefully and purposefully through a variety of exercises during the day. The variety of choices allows the children to find work which supports the task of childhood: building the human person. Imagine, now, a Montessori environment that includes work which also supports the children's relationship with God. This is the environment in Montessori schools affiliated with particular religions, including Christian Family Montessori School in Mount Rainer, MD, where my own children were students and where I work as the Director of Religious Education.

The parents at Christian Family Montessori School have chosen a school that will nurture their children's spiritual life, as Christians, as well as their physical, academic and cultural growth. By creating an environment that addresses the development of the whole child, we hope to avoid a false division between the secular and the spiritual. All of life can be holy. And children working with their bodies, minds, and spirits are working in communion with God.

The area of the classroom set aside for religious materials is called the *atrium*. The term was chosen by Maria Montessori because in the early church the atrium was a place set aside for the preparation of new

Christians for Baptism. Our atrium is similar to the rest of the Montessori environment in that it contains a choice of manipulative materials stored on low shelves. The source of these materials, however, is not math or language but the Bible and liturgy. The atrium also includes a place set aside for prayer — a small table to which one or more children can come to pray. On this table are objects such as a Bible, a candle, a plant, and a piece of religious art to support the children's prayer.

Montessori herself began to create materials to nurture the spiritual life of young children. In Rome, Sofia Cavalletti and Gianna Gobbi have continued to develop this aspect of Montessori's work. Dr. Cavalletti is a scholar of Hebrew scriptures and Ms. Gobbi in her early years studied personally with Dr. Montessori.

In 1954 Cavalletti and Gobbi together began to work with young children to develop a curriculum now known as *The Catechesis of the Good Shepherd*. The Good Shepherd is the image of Christ from the Bible which best corresponds to the spiritual life of young children. *Catechesis* means religious formation, based on the root word "echo", and refers to all the ways one's faith can be echoed at home, church, Sunday school, and throughout one's culture. The derivative word, *catechist* refers to the teacher or guide who presents this program to the children.

Using a creative procedure similar to that of Maria Montessori, Gobbi and Cavalletti developed *The Catechesis* by making materials, introducing them to the children, and then carefully observing the work of the children to determine if the materials met their needs. Appropriate materials had to meet three criteria. First, Cavalletti and Gobbi wanted materials that would invite the children to work with concentration and peace. Second, they wanted the children's work with the material to leave them feeling satisfied and joyful. This response would indicate that their deep needs were being met. Finally, they wanted materials that the children were eventually able to interpret through prayer, movement, conversation or art. This interpretation indicated that they did not merely memorize and repeat the content but actually internalized and connected it to their life experiences.

Some materials that met these three criteria include a model altar and all the articles used in the Mass to allow the children to learn the names and uses of these objects normally seen only from a distance in the hands of the priest; a topographical map of the Land of Israel to help the children connect Jesus to a real place; figures and houses that represent events surrounding the birth of Jesus, the Last Supper, and the Resurrection; figures representing some of Jesus' parables, especially the Good Shepherd, the Found Sheep and the Pearl of Great Price; and the water, candles and oils used at Baptism that communicate the meaning of Baptism to the children.

Cavelletti and Gobbi have been working with Roman Catholic children, but since they have focused on themes that are very basic to Christianity generally, some other Christian denominations have adapted *The Catechesis of the Good Shepherd* for use in religious education programs around the United States.[1] The Catechesis has also been used in Mexico, Canada, Brazil, Columbia, Australia, Chad and throughout Europe. Its use internationally indicates both its grounding in the universal spiritual needs of the child and the fact that experience with children from many nations has contributed to this universality.

THE FOUR ASPECTS OF SPIRITUALITY AS NURTURED BY
The Catechesis of The Good Shepherd

In Chapter Two of this book, the author highlights four aspects of spirituality: awe and wonder, openness to an existence beyond our sensory experience, humility, and oneness with the universe. The exercises she then offers in Part Three can help children to deepen these aspects of their spiritual life. But materials which are based on the "good news" of a particular faith tradition may provide even richer nourishment for the spirit because they can be specific. The following examples show how we nurture these four aspects of spirituality in the Christian tradition by using materials from *The Catechesis of the Good Shepherd.*

The first aspect, awe and wonder, is characterized by a reverence for the earth and all its creatures and a desire to live in harmony with all of nature.

---

[1] *The Catechesis of the Good Shepherd* has been adapted for use in Episcopal, Lutheran, Dutch Reformed, Baptist, Orthodox Catholic and Presbyterian churches. The method has the potential for adaptation for use in other religions as well, following the process of observation used by Montessori, Cavalletti and Gobbi.

A material that nourishes the sense of wonder is a small white container of mustard seeds the size of coarsely ground pepper. Jesus used these seeds to help his followers grasp the mystery of the growth of the reign of God because they are the smallest of any seeds at the time of their sowing (Mark 4, 30-32). In order to reflect on the reign of God, we stop to enjoy the miracle of the mustard seed itself.

It is so tiny and still. Yet it contains the most wonderful power: the power to grow into a large tree, a tree that shelters the birds of the air. Where does this power come from? How does it work? Can it be controlled? To whom, or to what, does it belong? What could we call it? The power of God? The strength of God? Life?

And where else do we see this wonderful power at work? We think of all the seeds throughout the earth, growing and growing. Imagine how much power they have together. We see it also in ourselves: we grow too. Does the power belong to us? And after we have reached our full height do we continue to grow? In what ways?

With questions like these we explore the mystery of the tiny mustard seeds, ending with a solemn reading of Jesus' own words from the Bible about them. Finally we ask, "What can these mustard seeds tell us about the kingdom of God?"

When five year old Gregory heard for the first time the question, "Where is this strength of God at work?" He answered with a huge grin, "In us!" Other children in the group named various plants and animals while Gregory continued to exclaim with delight, "In us!"

Children like Gregory perceive and help us to rejoice in the wonderful gift of life given to animals, plants, and all of creation, as well as to humankind. Children's affinity and love for creation is quite natural; they are spiritual people. Parables such as the mustard seed can deepen and bring to a more conscious level their inborn sense of wonder.

The second aspect of spirituality is openness to an existence that is beyond our sensory and intellectual experience. Wolf speaks of a "mystical leap." The ground from which we make this "mystical leap" is our sensory experience. We leap into the mystery of the reign of God from our contemplation of the mustard seed which we can see and feel. Cavalletti has found that children "move with ease in the world of the transcendent."[2]

Many of the materials of *The Catechesis of the Good Shepherd* establish a sensorial experience that is then linked to a religious mystery. Jesus used this approach with the parables, and the church continues the method with the liturgy. When a congregation gathers, their liturgy is full of gestures, objects, or words which serve as symbols of the metaphysical. Bread and wine, for example, which can be seen, smelled, felt and tasted, become in the liturgy a sign of the presence of Christ among us.

During a liturgy these symbols pass before the child rapidly and at a distance from the altar. In the atrium, they are introduced one at a time, with objects the children can handle, movements they can repeat, and words they can hear slowly and clearly.

For example, at the heart of the liturgy are the words of Jesus at the Last Supper before his death: over the bread he said, "This is my body which is given for you"; over the wine he said, "This is my blood which is shed for you." We introduce these words in their historical context with a miniature plate and cup, a small model of the dining table and figures of Jesus and his disciples. As the children connect this meal to communion at church they are more likely to speak of communion as "Jesus" than as "bread" because they are open to the metaphysical and are agile in making the "mystical leap."

The third aspect of spirituality is that it fosters a profound humility in human beings.

Before offering wine at a Catholic liturgy, the priest or deacon adds a few drops of water. In the atrium, the catechist slowly pours wine into a glass chalice, adds a drop of water and says, "The wine represents Jesus, the water represents us." The children consider what happened to the water. Where did it go? Can it be taken back out? Why do we add only a few drops? After introducing this brief gesture in the atrium, the catechist invites the children to repeat it at their leisure, as often as they would like. While working, the children consider the mystery of our union

---

[2] Sofia Cavalletti, *The Religious Potential of the Child*, p. 44.

with God who is so much greater than us. After almost a full year of repeating the gesture, a seven year old Italian boy said, "A few drops of water and a lot of wine, because we must lose ourselves in Jesus."[3]

Humility is the recognition that although we are much smaller than God, we are nevertheless important to and well loved by God. The parable of the Found Sheep helps the children to grasp this aspect of humility (Luke 15, 4-6). A shepherd of a large number of sheep will leave them to find just one that is lost. In like manner, God searches for us until we are found. Why does the shepherd search for the sheep? "Because he loves her," answer children of all ages.

Our atrium has a small round sheepfold on a table. This fence on a green wooden base has a gate that opens and closes. With it is a model of the Good Shepherd and ten sheep. The children bring the figures in and out of the sheepfold, lose one sheep by hiding it or placing it a short distance from the sheepfold, and move the shepherd to search for and find it again. They find at the same time a deep sense of their own great value as beloved children of God.

Finally, spirituality implies a sacred connection with all of life and a oneness with the universe, and therefore summons us to the highest of human virtues.

The children's work with the materials and prayer in the atrium deepens the sacred connection, the relationship with God and all of creation, without explicit moral teaching before the age of six. After the age of six, when the child enters the stage of moral development, we add materials based on the parables and teachings of Jesus that will help the child discover the moral implications of relationships.

Wolf states that our sense of connection precedes the summons to virtue. Cavalletti confirms this, writing, "The adult who wants to give children a moral formation...should announce God's love and help the child to experience and enjoy it in reflection and prayer."[4]

A parable that affirms the sacred connection is the True Vine (John 15, 1-11). In this parable, Jesus compares himself with a vine, saying, "I am the vine, you are the branches." As a catechist, I have asked six and

[3] Ibid p. 92.
[4] Ibid p. 153.

seven year olds who they think are the branches of this vine. Unlike adults who may limit "membership" to Christians, or to a particular denomination, children respond firmly, "everyone." People of every religion, every culture, every age are included. I asked about people who have died, and one girl said, "They are still on the vine because of the sap, the sap doesn't die." (In this discussion the children had decided the sap represents God's life flowing through the branches.)

The children often choose this parable to read at the celebration of their first communion, because it expresses so well their sense that communion means unity with God, all people and all of creation. In this spirit they eagerly participate in ecological projects such as recycling. They spontaneously think of ways to respond to the needs of people caught in tragedies around the world. They refuse to exclude anyone from their image of the true vine. Their sense of unity is deep, one that adults would do well to emulate rather than undermine.

How do we help children move from their sense of the sacred connection to living the "highest of human virtue"? The ability to judge right and wrong objectively (conscience) begins to develop about age six. The presentation of moral parables and maxims assists the growth of that ability.

The Good Samaritan is one of the first moral parables we explore (Luke 10, 30-37). We use small moveable wooden figures of the characters in the story to present this parable. As the children work with the material, acting out the robbery of the Jew and his rescue by a Samaritan thought to be an enemy, they consider some of the questions posed in the presentation. Did the Good Samaritan know the injured man might be his enemy? Then why did he stop? What was more important than the man being a possible enemy? What helped him to make the decision to stop? Why did the other travelers pass by the injured man? Who were they thinking about? What was Jesus trying to teach us with this story? In the same manner, the children reflect on other moral parables, including The Ten Bridesmaids, The Wedding Feast, The Insistent Friend, and The Pharisee and the Tax Collector.

Maxims are some of Jesus' short commands, including, "Love your enemy" (Matthew 5, 44), "Do good to those who hate you" (Matthew 5, 44) and "Love one another as I have loved you" (John 13, 24). They are written on separate wooden tablets and kept together in a beautiful box. The children choose them to copy and illustrate, often interpreting a maxim as they work. For example, one child wrote, "Love one another as I have loved you," and added a sketch of the birth of Christ at the bottom of her paper.

After the moral parables and maxims become part of the children's moral compass, they are applied to the choices of daily life by the children themselves. Following Montessori's example, the adult does not use the parables and maxims as rules to discipline children, but as tools handed to the children to learn to discipline themselves.

Children bring to the classroom and to the atrium a great wealth of spirit. Adults who are helping children often find themselves receiving spiritual gifts in return. Among them are children's understanding that the relationship with God is joyful rather than dutiful, that people and creation are deeply united in their life in God, and the announcements at the heart of our faith encourage and unite us rather than discourage and divide.

As you seek to nurture the spiritual life of young children, allow them to guide you as well into deep enjoyment of God and God's creation, lingering with them in awe and wonder and peace.[5]

---

[5] For further information about *The Catechesis of the Good Shepherd* write to: Center For Children and Theology, 3628 Rhode Island Avenue, Mount Rainier, MD 20712 or The Catechesis of the Good Shepherd, P. O. Box 1084, Oak Park, IL 60304.

Bibliography and Recommended Resources

Bibliography

Appelhof, Mary. *Worms Eat My Garbage.* Kalamazoo, MI: Flower Press, 1982.

Armstrong, Karen. *A History of God.* New York: Ballantine Books, 1993.

Bennett, J.G, et al. *The Spiritual Hunger of the Modern Child.* Charles Town, WV: Claymont Communications, 1984.

Berends, Polly Berrien. *Whole Child/Whole Parent.* New York: Harper and Row, 1983.

Burnett, Walt, (ed.). *The Human Spirit.* London: George Allen and Unwin Ltd., 1960.

Buscaglia, Leo. *Personhood.* Columbine, NY: Fawcett, 1978.

_____. *The Fall of Freddie the Leaf.* New York: Holt, Rinehart and Winston, 1982.

Campbell, Joseph with Bill Moyers. *The Power of Myth.* New York: Doubleday, 1988.

Carr, Rachael. *Be a Frog, Be a Bird, Be a Tree.* Garden City, NY: Doubleday, 1973.

Carson, Rachael. *The Sense of Wonder.* New York: Harper and Row, 1956.

Carter, Forrest. *The Education of Little Tree.* Albuquerque, NM: University of New Mexico Press, 1976 (Paperback 1986).

Cavalletti, Sofia. *The Religious Potential of the Child.* Chicago, IL: Liturgy Training Publications, 1992.

_____. *The Spiritual Development of the Child.* Montessori Talks to Parents. Cleveland Heights, OH: North American Montessori Teacher's Association, 1978.

Cherry, Clare. *Think of Something Quiet.* Belmont, CA: Pittman Learning Inc., 1981.

Clevenger, Kitty. *The Magic of Children.* Kansas City, MO: Hallmark Cards, 1971.

Coles, Robert. *The Spiritual Life of Children.* Boston: Houghton Mifflin Co., 1990.

Cornell, Joseph. *Sharing Nature With Children.* Nevada City, CA: Dawn Publications, 1979.

Covey, Stephen R. *The 7 Habits of Highly Effective People.* New York: Simon & Schuster, 1989.

Dewey, John. *Human Nature and Conduct; an Introduction to Social Psychology.* New York: The Modern Library, Random House, 1930.

Dillard, Annie. *An American Childhood.* New York: Harper and Row, 1987.

Fay, Martha. *Do Children Need Religion?* New York: Pantheon Books, 1993.

Fisher, Mary. *Sleep With The Angels: A Mother Challenges AIDS.* Wakefield, RI: Moyer Bell, 1994.

Fitzpatrick, Jean Grasso. *Something More.* New York: Viking, 1991.

Flake, Carol L. *Holistic Education: Principles, Perspectives and Practices.* Brandon, VT: Holistic Education Press, 1993.

Fletcher, Ruth. *Teaching Peace.* San Francisco: Harper and Row, 1986.

Frasier, Debra. *On The Day You Were Born.* New York: Harcourt Brace Jovanovich, 1991.

Gang, Philip S., Nina Myerhof Lynn and Dorothy J. Maver. *Conscious Education.* Atlanta: Dagaz Press, 1992.

Garth, Maureen. *Starbright Meditations for Children.* New York: Harper Collins Publisher, 1991.

Griffiths, Bede. *The Marriage of East and West.* Springfield, IL: Templegate Publishers, 1982.

Harris, Thomas. *I'm OK, You're OK.* A Practical Guide to Transactional Analysis. New York: Harper and Row, 1969.

Herzog, Stephanie. *Joy in the Classroom.* Boulder Creek, CA: University of the Trees Press, 1982.

James, Muriel, and Dorothy Jongeward. *Born to Win.* New York: The New American Library, Inc., 1978.

Janke, Rebecca, and Julie Peterson. *Peacemaker's A,B,C's for Young Children.* Growing Communities for Peace, 16542 Orwell Road North, Marine on St. Croix, MN. 55047, 1995.

Jung, C. G. *Modern Man in Search of a Soul.* New York: Harcourt Brace Jovanich, 1993.

_____. *Man and His Symbols.* New York: Dell Publishing Co., 1968.

_____. *The Integration of the Personality.* London: Routledge and Kegan Paul, Ltd., 1940.

Kelley, Kevin W. *The Home Planet.* New York: Addison Wesley, 1988.

Kramer, Rita. *Maria Montessori; a Biography.* New York: G.P. Putnam's Sons, 1976.

L'Engle, Madeleine. *A Circle of Quiet.* San Francisco: Harper, 1972.

Leopold, Aldo. *A Sand County Almanac.* New York: Oxford University Press, 1949.

McFarland, Sonnie. *Shining Through.* Denver: Shining Mountain Center, 1993.

Maslow, Abraham. *The Farther Reaches of Human Nature.* New York: Viking Press, 1971.

_____. *Religious Values and Peak Experiences.* New York: Viking Press, 1994.

Montessori, Maria. *The Absorbent Mind.* New York: Dell Publishing, 1967.

_____. *The Secret of Childhood.* Madras: Orient Longmans, 1936.

_____. *The Secret of Childhood.* Notre Dame, IN: Fides Publishers, Inc., 1966.

_____. *Education For a New World.* Adyar, Madras, India: Kalakshetra Publications, 1946.

_____. *The Discovery of the Child.* Adyar, Madras, India: Kalakshetra Publications, 1948.

_____. *From Childhood to Adolescence.* New York: Schocken Books, 1948.

_____. *To Educate the Human Potential.* Adyar Madras, India: Kalakshetra Publications, 1948.

_____. *The Montessori Method.* New York: Schocken Books, 1964.

_____. *Education and Peace.* Chicago: Henry Regnery and Co., 1972.

_____. *Peace and Education.* Madras: The Theosphical Publishing House, 1965.

Moore, Thomas. *Care of the Soul.* New York: Harper Collins, 1993.

Myers, Isabel Briggs with Peter B. Myers. *Gifts Differing.* Palo Alto, CA: Consulting Psychologists Press, 1980.

Nhat Hanh, Thich. *Peace In Every Step.* New York: Bantam Books, 1991.

Neihardt, John G. *Black Elk Speaks.* Lincoln, NE: University of Nebraska Press, 1932. (Bison Book, 1988)

Palmer, Parker J. *A Place Called Community.* Philadelphia, PA: Pendle Hill, 1977.

Pattell-Gray, Anne. *Through Aboriginal Eyes.* Geneva: WCC Publications, 1991.

Pearce, Joseph Chilton. *Evolution's End.* San Francisco: Harper, 1992.

Peck, M. Scott. *A Different Drum.* New York: Simon and Schuster, 1987.

Richter, Betts. *Something Special Within.* Marina del Ray, CA: Devorss and Company, 1978.

Rohr, Richard and Andreas Ebert. *Discovering The Enneagram.* New York: The Crossroad Publishing Co., 1993.

Standing, E.M. (ed.). *The Child in the Church.* St. Paul, MN: Catechetical Guild, 1965.

_____. *Maria Montessori Her Life and Work.* New York: American Library, 1962.

Swimme, Brian. *The Universe is a Green Dragon.* Santa Fe, NM: Bear and Co., 1984.

Teilhard de Chardin, Pierre. *Building the Earth.* Wilkes Barre, PA: Dimension Books, 1965.

Thrush, Ursula. *Peace 101.* 678 Portola Drive, San Francisco, CA 94127, 1992.

Trudeau, Sister Christina Marie, S.N.D. de N. *Montessori's Years in India.* Honolulu: Montessori Association of Hawaii, 1984.

Varley, Susan. *Badger's Parting Gifts.* New York: Lothrop, Lee and Shepherd, 1984.

Viorst, Judith. *The 10th Good Thing About Barney.* Tappan, NJ: Simon and Schuster Children's Group, 1971.

Wachtel, Paul L. *The Poverty of Affluence,* Philadelphia: New Society Publishers, 1989.

Westley, Dick. *Good Things Happen, Experiencing Community in Small Groups.* Mystic, CT: Twenty-third Publications, 1992.

Wolf, Aline D. *Child-Size Masterpieces.* Hollidaysburg, PA: Parent Child Press, 1986-1992.

Wolpe, Rabbi David J. *Teaching Your Children About God, A Modern Approach.* New York: Henry Holt and Sons, 1993.

Recommended Resources

All books are for children except where indicated.

Chapter 6   NOURISHING THE SPIRIT OF THE TEACHER

For All That Lives With The Words of Albert Schweitzer. Ann Atwood and Erica Anderson. New York: Charles Scribner's Sons. (adult)

Handbook for the Soul. Richard Carlson and Benjamin Shield, editors. Boston: Little, Brown and Company. (adult)

The Road Less Traveled. M. Scott Peck. New York: Simon and Schuster. (adult)

Chapter 9   CULTIVATING STILLNESS

Welcoming Babies. Margy Burns Knight. Gardiner, ME: Tilbury House Publishers.

Your Own Best Secret Place. Byrd Baylor and Peter Parnale. New York: Charles Scribner's Sons.

Chapter 10   WONDER — THE LEAVEN OF SPIRITUALITY

The Animal Atlas (A Pictorial Atlas of World Wildlife). Barbara Taylor. New York: Alfred A. Knopf, Inc.

And So They Build. Bert Kitchen. Cambridge, MA: Candlewick Press.

Hug a Tree and Other Things to do Outdoors With Young Children. Rockwell, Sherwood and Williams. (adult)

In the Small, Small Pond. Denise Fleming. New York: Henry Holt and Company.

In the Tall, Tall Grass. Denise Fleming. New York: Henry Holt and Company.

Listening to Nature. Joseph Cornell. Nevada City, CA: Dawn Publications. (adult)

Once There Was a Tree. Natalia Romanova. New York: Dial Books.

Owl Moon. Jane Yolen. New York: Scholastic Press.

Chapter 12   THE SPIRITUAL MEANING OF COSMIC EDUCATION

All I See is Part of Me. Chara M. Curtis. Bellevue, WA: Illumination Arts.

Space Age. William J. Walter, New York: Random House. (adult)

The Universe Story. Brian Swimme and Thomas Berry. San Francisco: Harper. (adult)

Chapter 13   CARE OF THE EARTH — A SPIRITUAL WAY OF LIFE

Brother Eagle, Sister Sky. Susan Jeffers. New York: Dial Books.

The Dream of the Earth. Thomas Berry. San Francisco: Sierra Club Books. (adult)

The Spiritual Legacy of the American Indian. Joseph Epes Brown. New York, NY: Crossroad. (adult)

The Earth and I. Frank Asch. San Diego: A Gulliver Green Book, Harcourt Brace Jovanovich.

Earth Child. Kathryn Sheehan and Mary Waidner. Tulsa, OK: Council Oak Books. (adult)

Earth Prayers, edited by Elizabeth Roberts and Elias Amidon. New York: Harper Collins. (adult)

I Was Good to the Earth Today. Susan Bryer Starr. Rohnert Park, CA: Starhouse Publishing.

The Indian Way. Gary McLain. (ages 8 and up). Santa Fe, NM. John Muir Publications.

Teaching Kids to Love the Earth,(Sharing a Sense of Wonder - *186 Outdoor Activities for Parents and Other Teachers).* Marina C. Herman, Joseph E. Passineau, Ann L. Schimpf and Paul Treuer. Duluth, MN: Pfiefer-Hamilton Publishers. (adult)

Chapter 14   THE SPIRITUAL ROOTS OF PEACE EDUCATION

Love is Letting Go of Fear. Gerald G. Jampolsky, MD. New York: Bantam Books. (adult)

Peaceful Children, Peaceful World. Aline Wolf. Hollidaysburg, PA: Parent Child Press. (adult)

Chapter 15   CHILDREN'S INNER PEACE AND LOVE

Discover the World: Helping Children Develop Respect for Themselves, Others, and the Earth, edited by Susan Hopkins and Jeffrey Winters. Philadelphia: The New Society Publishers. (adult)

Here a Little Child I Stand. Satomi Ichikawa. New York: Philomel Books.

Just Because I Am. Lauren Murphy Payne. Minneapolis, MN: Free Spirit Publishers.

Meditation for Children. Deborah Rozman, Ph.D., Boulder Creek, CA: Aslan Publishing, University of the Trees Press. (adult)

Peace Begins With You. Katherine Scholes. San Francisco: Sierra Club Books / Little, Brown and Company.

Peace on Earth. Bijou Le Tord. New York: Doubleday.

Spinning Inward. Maureen Murdock, Boston: Shambhala Publications, Inc. (adult)

Yoga for Children. Erene Cheki Haney and Ruth Richards. New York: Bobbs-merrill Co., Inc. (adult)

Chapter 16   PEACE IN THE CLASSROOM COMMUNITY

Black Elk, a Man With a Vision. Carol Greene. Chicago: Children's Press.

The Children's Book of Virtues. William J. Bennett. New York: Simon and Schuster.

Kids' Random Acts of Kindness. Foreward by Rosalynn Carter. Berkeley, CA: Conari Press.

Learning Skills of Peacemaking. Naomi Drew. Rolling Hills Estates, CA: Jalmar Press. (adult)

Our Peaceful Classroom. Aline Wolf. Hollidaysburg, PA: Parent Child Press.

Peace Prayers. edited by Carrie Leadingham, et al. New York: Harper Collins. (adult)

Peacemaking For Little Friends. Mary Joan Park. Mount Rainier, MD: Little Friends for Peace. (adult)

Secret of the Peaceful Warrior. Dan Millman. Tiburon, CA: H.J. Kramer, Inc., Starseed Press.

Starting Out Right. Kathleen McGinnis and Barbara Oehlberg. New York: The Crossword Publishing Co. (adult)

The Story of the Jumping Mouse. John Steptoe. New York: Lothrop, Lee and Shepard Books.

Chapter 17   THE SCHOOL AS A FAMILY/GLOBAL COMMUNITY

All God's Critters Got a Place in the Choir. Bill Staines. New York: Penguin Books.

The Big Book of Peace. Lloyd Alexander, et al. New York: Dutton Children's Books.

The Butter Battle Book. Dr. Seuss. New York: Random House.

Celebrations of Life. Muysa Meyer and Tim Seldin. Silver Spring, MD: The Barrie Press. (adult)

Children Just Like Me (a Unique Celebration of Children Around the World). Barnabas and Anabel Kindersley. New York: Dorling Kindersley Publishing Co.

Global Child (Multicultural Resource for Young Children). Maureen Cech. CA: Addison-Wesley Publishing Co. (adult)

Kwanzaa. Deborah Newton Chocolate. Chicago: Children's Press.

My Friends Live in Many Places. Dorka Raynor. Chicago: Albert Whitman and Company.

My World/Peace. edited by Richard and Helen Exley. Lincolnwood, IL: Passport Books.

Sadako and the Thousand Paper Cranes. Eleanor Coerr. New York: Dell Publishing.

Straight to the Heart. Ethan Hubbard. Post Mills, VT: Chelsea Green Publishing Co.

The White Feather. Ruth Eitzen. Scottsdale, PA: Herald Press.

Chapter 18   SPIRITUALITY AND THE ARTS

I Am An Artist. Pat Lowery Collins. Brookfield, CT: The Millbrook Press.

A Child's Book of Art (Great Pictures, First Words). Selected by Lucy Mickiethwait. New York: Dorling Kindersley Publishing, Inc.

Come Look With Me (a series of four books). Gladys S. Blizzard. Charlottesville, VA: Thomasson-Grant.

The Children's Year. Stephanie Cooper et al. Gloucestershire, UK: Hawthorn House.

Good Earth Art. (Environmental Art for Kids, Mary Ann F. Kohl and Cindy Gainer. (adult)

Pass It On, African American Poetry for Children. New York: Scholastic, Inc..

Let Out the Sunshine — A Montessori Approach to Creative Activities, by Regina Reynolds Barnett, Dubuque, Iowa: Wm. C. Brown Company Publishers, 1981.

Chapter 20   WHAT ABOUT GOD?

Answers to a Child's Questions About Death. Peter Stillman. Stanford, NY: Guideline Publications.

Old Turtle. Douglas Wood. Duluth, MN: Pfeifer-Hamilton Publishers.

What Is God? Etan Boritzer. Willowdale, Ontario, CANADA: Firefly Books, Ltd.

Prayer is Reaching. Howard Bogot and Daniel B. Syme. New York: Union of American Hebrew Congregations.

Themes in Religion. Clive Erricker, editor. (Series includes Buddhism, Christianity, Hinduism, Islam, Judaism, Sikhism.) Essex CM202JE, England: Longman Group.